# Ending child poverty by 2020

## The first five years

D1438183

**Edited by Paul Dornan**

CPAG • 94 White Lion Street • London N1 9PF

CPAG promotes action for the relief, directly or indirectly, of poverty among children and families with children. We work to ensure that those on low incomes get their full entitlements to welfare benefits. In our campaigning and information work we seek to improve benefits and policies for low-income families in order to eradicate the injustice of poverty. If you are not already supporting us, please consider making a donation, or ask for details of our membership schemes and publications.

Poverty Publication 110

Published by CPAG
94 White Lion Street, London N1 9PF

© CPAG 2004

ISBN 1 901698 72 6

The views expressed in this book are the authors' and do not necessarily express those of CPAG.

A CIP record for this book is available from the British Library.

Cover and design by Devious Designs 0114 275 5634
Typeset by Boldface 020 7833 8868
Printed by Russell Press 0115 978 4505

# Contents

# Acknowledgements

I would like to thank all the authors for so generously giving up their time to contribute to this publication. Thanks are also due to Geoff Fimister and Adrian Sinfield for their comments.

Thanks are also due to Alison Key for editing and managing the production of the book and to Paula McDiarmid for proofreading the text.

*Paul Dornan*

# About the contributors

**Pete Alcock** is Professor of Social Policy and Administration and Head of the School of Social Sciences at the University of Birmingham.

**Paul Dornan** is the Policy Officer at Child Poverty Action Group.

**Lisa Harker** is the Chair of the Daycare Trust.

**Ruth Lister** is Professor of Social Policy at Loughborough University.

**Alan Marsh** is Professor of Social Policy at the University of Westminster and the Deputy Director of the Policy Studies Institute.

**Tess Ridge** is the Principal Policy and Practice Officer at Barnardo's.

**Neera Sharma** is a Research Officer in the Centre for the Analysis of Social Policy at the University of Bath.

**Sandra Vegeris** is a Research Fellow at the Policy Studies Institute.

# Introduction
*Paul Dornan*

On 18 March 1999 Prime Minister Tony Blair used the following words in a speech at Toynbee Hall in East London.

> Our historic aim, that ours is the first generation to end child poverty forever... It's a 20-year mission, but I believe it can be done.[1]

It is five years since Tony Blair made that commitment and we have reached the first milestone year (2004/05) on route. It is a good time to evaluate progress so far and to use this experience to see what more needs to be done. This is what this book seeks to do.

Within a generation – later interpreted as by 2020 – the Government was to have eradicated child poverty. For an organisation like Child Poverty Action Group, this is food and drink. It is a historic commitment and one that should be praised to the rafters. The detail of how we could get from a situation in which a baby born in Great Britain faced a one in three chance of being born into income poverty[2] to one in which a newborn would face, theoretically at least, no risk of poverty is more complex. The commentary and analysis within this book sheds light on this issue.

The progress made has been encouraging. Income poverty has been falling – from a risk of 34 to 30 per cent. The four percentage point difference does not sound much, but it equates to 500,000 children. This progress against the income poverty targets is examined in the final conclusion. That income poverty has fallen is a real success, especially given the background of increasing average wages and incomes that might have been expected to push things in the opposite direction. Alan Marsh and Sandra Vegeris give us evidence, which perhaps makes it easier to relate to the daily experiences of children – that severe hardship, based on an index of material items – has fallen. There has been progress and it demonstrates just what is possible from a committed government.

Tess Ridge starts us off in the first chapter with the voice of the child and provides an insight into the experiences of children born into families facing such income restraint. A related tone is struck by Ruth Lister in the penultimate chapter, in which she discusses the human rights of the child and how policy ought to treat children as children, not purely as a future workforce. Both contributions focus our attention on the impact that policy may have on the lives of children today.

The Government has sought to address the incomes of children and families through a variety of interventions. Alan Marsh and Sandra Vegeris discuss the work agenda, analysing recent data from the Family and Children Survey to show the role that it has played, alongside tax credits, in reducing severe hardship. Closely allied to this work agenda is the provision of good-quality affordable childcare, the lack of which is one major driver of worklessness. Lisa Harker analyses policy in this area and discusses what is needed, both to fulfil the employment agenda of the Government but also from the perspective of families. Poverty and social exclusion are often considered to have a spatial dimension, being demonstrably worse in some areas than others. For this reason we have seen numerous area-based initiatives spark under New Labour, including: the New Deal for Communities, action zones, Sure Start and the Children's Fund. Pete Alcock takes a look at the use of area-based initiatives, analysing the extent to which these are able to deal with poverty. He argues that there is certainly scope, but that this is limited by a lack of focus on individual income – people may be poor in areas not deemed so and hence area-based initiatives are not always well focused on the poorest. Neera Sharma picks up on this note by dealing with the social care agenda that seeks to improve the lives of the most vulnerable children in society. The policy focus is needed, but she shows how it must be more directed towards children at high risk of poverty. The book concludes with an evaluation of the progress thus far and a comment on the way forward.

In the run up to the 2001 general election, CPAG published *An End in Sight?*[3] This collection of essays by leading academics sought to analyse progress since 1997 in a variety of areas, focusing in particular on employment, education, health, housing, neighbourhood renewal and policies connected with race. The book ended with the following comment:

> Is there an end in sight for child poverty? Our society has the resources; we need only to maintain and strengthen the political will.[4]

Three years further down the track, the broad conclusion from the contributions in this book does not differ from that of *An End in Sight?*. There are three headline messages. First, reducing and ending child poverty is vital for the effectiveness, as well as the justice, of UK society. Secondly, the current administration has achieved much. It has raised the profile of the issue and, through redistributive policy, has reduced the risk of income poverty and hardship faced by children. This should be welcomed warmly. Finally, looking towards the future, if we are to end child poverty, we need more discussion and more redistribution focused on income-poor families.

## Notes

1   Reproduced in R Walker (ed), *Ending Child Poverty, popular welfare for the 21st century?*, The Policy Press, 1999

2   As defined as living in a household with a needs-adjusted income of below 60 per cent of the median, after housing costs. National Statistics, *Households Below Average Income: an analysis of the income distribution from 19949/5 – 2001/02*, Department for Work and Pensions, 2003

3   G Fimister (ed), *An End in Sight? Tackling child poverty in the UK*, Child Poverty Action Group, 2001

4   See note 3, p105

# One

# Putting children first: Addressing the needs and concerns of children who are poor

*Tess Ridge*

Five years ago, Tony Blair committed his government to a long-term policy goal: the eradication of childhood poverty in 20 years. This radical pledge has the potential to transform the lives and experiences of low-income and disadvantaged children in the UK. Labour's focus on children has succeeded in bringing the issue of childhood poverty out from the political shadows and into the public spotlight. Furthermore, placing the needs of low-income children at the centre of the policy-making agenda has served to highlight the great disparities in health, wealth, education and opportunity that exist between children in different social and economic circumstances.[1] This new political commitment to improve children's lives also presents us with an opportunity to explore how we as a society value children and the quality of childhood that we would want them to enjoy. Labour's interest in the lives of children is very welcome and continuing support for children and their families is essential if childhood poverty is to become a thing of the past. However, despite increased policy attention and the redistribution of resources towards children, there is still some way to go before the needs and concerns of children who are poor are truly addressed.

At present to achieve its aim of eradicating child poverty within 20 years and halving it by 2010, the Government has instituted a radical programme of welfare reform, which has fundamentally changed the way children are supported by the state.[2] This has meant a plethora of anti-poverty measures directed towards children and their families. Some of these, such as Sure Start, have a clear child focus and others such as New Deal for Lone Parents, are directed at their parents and driven by a wider range of policy agendas, including welfare to work and labour market concerns.[3] The scope and diversity of anti-poverty measures reflect the tensions that exist between the interests of the state and the rights and responsibilities of parents. In this policy environment the needs and concerns of children themselves can easily be overlooked. When children have been the central focus of anti-poverty policies, the measures proposed have tended to be directed towards children as adults of the future, rather than as children with their own issues and concerns. This focus on children as adults-to-be is heightened by the emergence of a new 'social investment state' where the state's interest in children as citizen-workers of the future is a key feature.[4] However, this future orientation in policy neglects the concerns and experiences of childhood itself, and leads to policies that are formulated in particular ways, which ultimately are not concerned with providing better childhoods for children.[5]

## Children's experiences of poverty in childhood

Children experience poverty in the immediacy of childhood among their peers, and any policies which seek to address childhood poverty need to be centrally concerned with children's everyday lives and experiences, as well as maintaining a focus on ensuring positive outcomes for children in adulthood. Therefore, the Government needs to go further than statistical evidence and performance indicators, valuable though these are. It needs to develop an understanding of childhood poverty that is rooted in childhood and informed by children's accounts of their lives and experiences. Children who are poor are not a homogenous group, although they are often represented as being so. Their experiences of being poor will be mediated by, among other things, their age, gender, ethnicity, health and whether or not they are disabled. In addition, children will interpret their experiences of poverty in the context of a diverse range of social, geographical and cultural settings.

When we listen to the voices of children who are poor, it is apparent that poverty imposes severe economic, social and emotional pressures on children's lives.[6] Childhood is a socially demanding experience and the issues that children identify as important for them may not be those articulated by adults.[7] Fitting in and joining in with the accepted social and cultural practices of their peers is a significant issue for all children and no less so for children who are poor. Policies that are directed towards the eradication of childhood poverty without an understanding of some of these issues and concerns are in danger of failing children at critical periods of their lives. In the following sections research carried out with children and young people living in low-income and disadvantaged households is used to highlight some of the issues poor children themselves have identified as important for their lives and well-being.[8] These include economic and material worries, and concerns about social inclusion in schools. Setting these issues in the context of what is already being done, we ask whether and how the Government is responding to these subjective needs, and explore what more can be done to address them in the future.

## Children's economic and material worries

The Government has introduced a substantial range of anti-poverty policies, which provide a very welcome redistribution of resources towards children and their families. This enhanced support for children is evident in many policy areas and has taken many different forms, including increased investment in family policies and education.[9] In particular, they have radically overhauled financial support for children, raising the level of premiums for children in low-income working and non-working households, increasing support for children with disabilities and substantially uprating child benefit, an important element of children's welfare rights.[10] Furthermore, the introduction of the child tax credit signals a new and significant undertaking to support low-income children in the future, regardless of their parental employment status. These are significant and substantial economic measures that show a strong government commitment to the well-being of disadvantaged children.

Clearly, increased financial support for children has a valuable role to play in improving low-income children's lives and will go some way towards addressing children's fears about income inequalities and material deprivation. In their accounts of their lives children who are poor express significant concerns about money and whether or not their families have enough income to provide for their needs. They are also fearful about being singled out as different or excluded on the basis of being poor and unable to pay their way. Therefore, increasing income in families is a fundamental step towards improving children's lives and their overall financial security.

However, the Government has not increased adult income support premiums and this will inevitably lead to a dilution of the impact of increases for children, as the adult rate of income support is a more sub-stantial element of family income than the allowance for a child. Furthermore, many families with children are considerably burdened by debt repayments and have deductions from their weekly income support payments to pay utility bills and social fund loans. Although it is important to focus on the needs of children and see them as citizens in their own right, they cannot be divorced from their families. Children experience considerable concern for their parents and worry about their capacity to pay their bills and manage on a low income. Just as parents try to pro-tect their children from the worst effects of poverty, children also try to protect their parents from how poverty is affecting their everyday lives.[11] This can lead to children lowering their aspirations and moderating their desires in an attempt to lessen the pressures they feel poverty is exerting on their parents and their families.[12] Therefore, it is important to provide increased economic support for children within the context of their fami-ly lives, and this will mean raising the level of financial support we provide for their parents as well.

A further concern identified by children is lack of pocket money and adequate funds to ensure social participation and inclusion. This is a sig-nificant social issue for many children, but it is also a critical growth and development matter. In our increasingly complex economic world lack of experience in money management can severely inhibit the development of essential socio-economic skills. At present, many children respond to a lack of pocket money and autonomous income by working, often at a younger age than the legal age for paid employment. The new child trust fund is designed to respond to some of these issues by providing a sav-ings account for every child at birth, with extra payments made by the Government for low-income children.[13] This is a new approach to sup-port for children and it will be linked to socio-economic education in the classroom. However, although any investment in children is to be wel-comed, the child trust fund does not actually make any real difference to poor children's lives in childhood. Like many policies directed towards children, this policy is ultimately concerned with children as future adults and any benefits derived from the child trust fund will be felt in early adult-hood, at age 18 when young people are able to access their savings accounts. Furthermore, the provision of socio-economic education linked to the child trust fund is potentially problematic and divisive if children in more affluent families are able to generate considerably higher savings funds than those available to low-income children. These issues will have to be sensitively handled by schools to avoid stigma and feelings of difference. Yet, children's accounts of their school lives indicate that their experiences of school are often problematic and characterised by social and institutional exclusion.

## Children's concerns about social inclusion in schools

The importance of school in children's lives has been recognised by the Government and this is a key area of anti-poverty intervention. However, much of the Government's policy attention has been focused on literacy and numeracy targets, which are central elements of its project of addressing poor adult outcomes of spells of poverty in childhood. Policies have also been directed towards concerns about children and school attendance, including those that are focused on truancy and exclusion from school.[14] These are important areas for intervention and measures to address school exclusions are particularly valuable. However, considerably less attention has been paid to inclusion within school and the vital social role that school plays in children's lives. At present, the additional costs associated with children's education are rising and many families are finding it difficult to meet them; for low-income families the burden of extra school costs can be particularly acute.[15]

When children who are poor talk about their experiences at school they often highlight difficulties they are experiencing joining in with the social opportunities that their more affluent schoolmates are enjoying. This can mean exclusion from a range of social occasions. Many children report regularly missing out on school trips and excursions, because of the costs involved and a lack of concessions and financial support within their schools. For older children a particular cause for concern occurs when school trips are intended as opportunities to enhance overall understanding of exam subjects. It can also mean that children are missing out on valuable social interaction and the generation of shared memories and meanings.

Children also report problems gaining access to leisure clubs and other school activities, which cost money to join or need special clothes or equipment. There is some acknowledgement by the Government of these concerns and the new pupil learning credits, which are being piloted at present, are intended to help low-income children take part in clubs etc.[16] This is a very welcome initiative, but it will not address children's needs adequately if it is targeted only towards schools that have a high percentage of free school meal receipts. Rural low-income children in particular are unlikely to benefit from the policy, even though, paradoxically, they may be at great risk of stigma and exclusion within their schools, where poverty tends to be hidden and a minority experience.

The cost of school uniforms is another concern frequently voiced by children. Although school uniforms in general are seen as having a protective effect, if families are unable to afford to buy the uniform this protection is undermined and children can become fearful of being singled out and stigmatised for wearing inappropriate clothing. There is no longer a system of grants to help with the costs of buying school uniforms, and overall support for families in this area is patchy and inconsistent.[17] Yet this is a significant area of concern for children and many families on a low income are forced to take out social fund loans to buy clothing and school uniforms in an attempt to ensure that their children are not penalised or singled out in any way at school. This inevitably results in greater poverty, as weekly deductions are taken from benefits to repay the loans.

Measures to provide adequate non-stigmatised support for families facing difficulties affording school costs are essential if children's concerns about school inclusion are to be acknowledged. The social fund is often the first port of call for families struggling to meet the extra costs of childhood and it is in need of urgent reform if it is to play any part in providing sufficient or appropriate support for children. Increased funding for education is also essential if schools are to provide more equitable and inclusive educational opportunities. The restoration of the school uniform grant would also directly address children's fears of difference, and relieve some of the pressure on over-stretched family budgets.

The problems children identify with school inclusion and participation are important preoccupations for children; they represent the everyday minutiae of children's lives and relationships. We still know very little about how children mediate and interpret their experiences of poverty, and how those experiences impact on their future well-being and self-esteem. What we do know is that school is a key site of policy intervention where governments can make an important contribution towards improving the lives of children who are poor.[18] But, addressing childhood poverty and social exclusion through school requires policies that aim to embrace far more than improved attendance and increased standards of literacy and numeracy. Improving school life for low-income children is fundamentally linked to how children feel about their school environment, and their experiences of being socially included and valued within their schools.

## Looking to the future

Labour's commitment to eradicate child poverty and support family life has resulted in a significant redistribution of resources towards children and their families, and this is very welcome. However, eliminating childhood poverty is a difficult task and the challenge facing the Government now lies in how it will approach the next five years. Childhood is a period of intense social, emotional and physical development and a range of policies are needed which address issues that adults might not recognise or see as important, such as friendships, access to transport and social opportunities, as well as greater participation and inclusion within schools. Much of the Government's child poverty strategy has stressed the value of children as the adults of the future, and policies have been formulated to ensure that children are given 'the tools they will need to succeed in the adult world'.[19] Future government policies need to respond to the pressing issues and concerns of children who are poor now. To do so it is necessary to value childhood as an experience in and of itself and ensure that children are given the tools and support they need to succeed in the child world.

### Notes

1    Department of Social Security, *Opportunity for All: tackling poverty and social exclusion*, The Stationery Office, 1999; J Bradshaw (ed), *Poverty: the outcomes for children*, Family Policy Studies Centre, 2000; D Gordon, L Adelman, K Ashworth, J Bradshaw, J Levitas, S Middleton, C Pantazis, D Patsios, S Payne, P Townsend and J Williams, *Poverty and Social Exclusion in Britain*, Joseph Rowntree Foundation, 2000

2    T Ridge, 'Benefiting Children? The challenge of childhood poverty', in J Millar (ed), *Understanding Social Security: issues for social policy and practice*, The Policy Press, 2003

3    Department of Social Security, *Opportunity for All: tackling poverty and social exclusion*, The Stationery Office, 1999

4    R Lister, 'Investing in the Citizens-Workers of the Future: transformations in citizenship and the state under New Labour', *Social Policy and Administration* 37(5), 2003, pp427-43

5    A Prout, 'Children's Participation: control and self-realisation in British late modernity', *Children and Society* 14, 2000, pp304-15

6    S Middleton, K Ashworth and R Walker, *Family Fortunes*, Child Poverty Action Group, 1994; D Roker, *Worth More Than This: young people growing up in family poverty*, The Children's Society, 1998; T Ridge, *Childhood Poverty and Social Exclusion*, The Policy Press, 2002

7  J Ennew and V Morrow, 'Out of the Mouths of Babes', in E Verhellen and F Spiesschaert (eds), *Children's Rights Monitoring Issues*, Myes and Breesch, 1994; M Hill, 'What's the Problem? Who can Help? The perspectives of children and young people on their well-being and on helping professionals', *Journal of Social Work Practice* 13(2), 1999, pp135-45

8  See note 6

9  See note 3; J Millar and T Ridge, 'Parents, Children, Families and New Labour: developing family policy?', in M Powell (ed), *Evaluating New Labour's Welfare Reforms*, The Policy Press, 2002, pp85-106

10  HM Treasury, *Supporting Children Through the Tax and Benefit System*, HM Treasury, 1999; see note 2

11  See note 2

12  See note 2

13  HM Treasury, *Detailed Proposals for the Child Trust Fund*, The Stationery Office, 2003

14  Social Exclusion Unit, *Truancy and Schools Exclusion*, The Stationery Office, 1998

15  E Tanner, F Bennett, H Churchill, G Ferres, S Tanner and S Wright, *The Costs of Education: a local study*, Child Poverty Action Group, 2003

16  Department for Education and Skills, *Schools Building on Success*, The Stationery Office, 2001

17  *Uniform Failure: CAB clients' experiences of help with school uniform costs*, National Association of Citizens Advice Bureaux, 2001

18  T Cox (ed), *Combating Educational Disadvantage: meeting the needs of vulnerable children*, Falmer Press, 2000; I Nicaise (ed), *The Right to Learn: educational strategies for socially excluded youth in Europe*, The Policy Press, 2000

19  See note 3

# Two
# Spatial and community aspects

*Pete Alcock*

## The spatial dimension

Political and academic debate about poverty has traditionally largely focused upon attempts to define and measure who is poor and to develop and implement policies to combat or relieve poverty. The focus is thus upon who is poor and policy intervention is targeted at all the individuals or families falling within that definition. Given this, we might wonder why it is important in a book assessing the achievements of the Government in combating poverty to discuss the spatial dimension of poverty – to pose the question in a nutshell: why does it matter where people are poor?

In fact, it is not entirely true to suggest that analysis of poverty has not explored the issue of spatial distribution. CPAG itself published an important collection on the social geography of poverty in 1995, which discussed research evidence from geographers and others who had examined the uneven geographical distribution of poverty within the UK.[1] And their most important, and overriding, conclusion was that poverty was not evenly distributed, geographically-speaking – some parts of the country have more poor people than others. What is more, this is not a terribly new insight; another geographical collection published in 1979 discussed much the same issues, although it focused more directly upon cities and the urban dimension of poverty;[2] and this work itself drew on earlier American analyses of urban (or ghetto) poverty in the US in the 1960s.

What all of this establishes, however, is that poverty is differently distributed spatially, with concentrations in particular areas; and for some time this uneven spatial distribution has attracted the attention of policy makers. In simple terms the policy question that flows from this is whether, given spatial concentrations of poverty, it makes sense to target policy action onto poor areas, rather than poor people. Since, if many poor people are to be found in such areas, area improvements generated by such targeting are likely to provide a disproportionately beneficial impact on the local poor, and so reduce or alleviate more generally overall levels of poverty although, as we shall see, there are some contradictions inherent in such a targeted approach to anti-poverty policy.

Following this logic, area-based policy action has been developed and implemented by governments in the UK, and elsewhere for a number of decades, and much has been written by academics and researchers about the aims and impacts of these.[3] What is important about this in the context of this book, however, is that the spatial dimension of poverty and the commitment to target policy action onto poor areas in order to combat it has been one of the major policy priorities of the current Labour government. Labour has much expanded previous geographical targeting within anti-poverty strategy. It has increased the resources available for local policy action and has spread the range of activities which these are being used to support.

## Area-based initiatives

Area-based initiatives (ABIs) is the term used to describe this plethora of new programmes and projects to provide additional resources for combating the spatial concentrations of poverty found in Britain in the early twenty-first century. There is now an ABI website maintained by the Regional Co-ordination Unit of the Office of the Deputy Prime Minister (ODPM) providing information about the range of activities which lists around *fifty* separate initiatives (www.rcu.gov.uk/abi ). Indeed, the rapid growth in the range of ABIs has already begun to worry the Government; and, following a report from the Performance and Innovation Unit which expressed concern about the 'proliferation' of ABIs,[4] a formal review was carried out within the ODPM,[5] leading to the closure of some and the merger of others – already expansion is to some extent being reigned back.

The devolution of policy making to the Scottish Parliament and Welsh and Northern Ireland Assemblies has complicated the picture of policy practice across the UK. Many of the initiatives discussed here have been developed within England only, although there are similar, but distinct, developments taking place within the devolved administrations in the other countries within the UK. For the sake of brevity, much of the discussion here focuses upon activity in England, although in practice similar initiatives can be found in other devolved administrations.

In fact, the recent development of ABIs extends back to the local regeneration programmes of the previous Conservative administration. Of particular importance here was the Single Regeneration Budget (SRB), initiated under Major, but continued and extended by Labour into a £5.6 billion programme supporting up to 900 local schemes, although these are now being phased out, and they have been transferred to the new regional development agencies.

Since 1977, however, Labour has introduced a number of new programmes, including the health, education and employment action zones which commenced within the first year of office, the Sure Start and Children's Fund programmes (support for work with pre-school and school-age children), the New Deal for Communities and the Neighbourhood Renewal Fund, along with many more smaller and more focused programmes addressing issues such as community safety and environmental protection. Some of these, such as Sure Start, have also been rolled out within the devolved administrations and there has also been the development there of independent, but analogous initiatives, such as the Social Inclusion Partnership in Scotland.

Although this recent growth in area-based activity draws on the longer history of geographical targeting mentioned above, its current prominence is the product of its inter-relation with the Government's new policy pledges to reducing poverty and social exclusion – and the links between this and its more general championing of a 'third way' for policy planning, which focuses upon partnership and participation in policy delivery. It is not just a concern with *what* is done locally, but *how* it is done.

Critically important to this new policy drive is the concern with *social exclusion*, as well as (or even instead of) the more traditional problem of poverty. Without getting into a complex theoretical debate about the nature of social exclusion and its difference from poverty,[6] the Government takes it to mean more than just monetary or income inequality to include also issues such as health status, housing and environmental circumstances, access to and use of services, and much more. Combating social exclusion requires a wider range of policy actions and policy goals. For instance, over fifty indicators covering such issues are listed in the Government's annual reports on combating social exclusion.[7]

To recognise this, the Government also acted quickly to establish, early in 1998, a new policy agency: the Social Exclusion Unit (SEU). The SEU is an inter-departmental unit working directly to the Cabinet Office. It has no significant budget or personnel, being comprised mainly of staff seconded from service departments, and its remit is 'to co-ordinate and improve Government action' and ' to focus on areas where it can add value and address long-term causes'.[8] In recognition of the potentially limitless scale of this task, the Unit has been given a series of selective foci for its work, such as rough sleepers, teenage pregnancies and young run-aways.

One of its early concerns, however, was that of 'problem estates' and it was out of this that endorsement of area-based action to combat social exclusion emerged. In a series of papers discussing the evidence on spatial inequalities and the damaging consequences of neighbourhood decline, the SEU outlined the case for locally-based responses to social exclusion.[9] And as a direct result of this, the Government established the New Deal for Communities (NDC: £2 billion over ten years for project work in 39 target neighbourhoods) and the Neighbourhood Renewal Fund (NRF: £900 million over three years for the 88 most deprived local authority districts, to be spent on local action projects) in England. NDC and NRF are major planks in the ABI policy drive and clear examples of the links between policies to tackle spatial disparities in the distribution of poverty and the broader conception of social exclusion which underpin current policy planning. They have been replicated in the devolved administrations by initiatives such as the Scottish Social Inclusion Partnerships. They are also evidence of a 'third way' approach, based on the role of the SEU in promoting inter-agency collaboration and 'joined-up' policy practice and in invoking partnership and participation as the new means for policy delivery.

## The achievements of area-based activity

The scale and scope of area-based policy action across the UK is, in a sense, a policy achievement in itself. Resources are flowing into the poorest districts and neighbourhoods, and these are being targeted by new policy initiatives to address many of the most pressing aspects of poverty and deprivation being experienced there. All sorts of local projects, organisations and services have been developed and supported.[10] The SEU now publishes a regular newsletter (*Inclusion*) highlighting innovations and achievements, such as support for neighbourhood management schemes in areas of low-demand housing, the creation of a national domestic violence helpline and outreach work with young prostitutes. Sure Start, supporting work with pre-school children, now funds 524 local programmes, serving up to 400,000 children living in disadvantaged areas and providing a range of services from childminding and home-based childcare to community centres with crèches, playgroups, toy libraries, training and consultation provided by local care professionals, and links to other local projects such as money advice and credit unions. And in Scotland, a new initiative in 2004 will target £20 million into childcare projects which support access to education and employment.

Whilst some of these activities would no doubt have gone ahead anyway (indeed, sometimes ABI resources are sustaining existing organisations or activities), there is no doubt that the scale and scope of such local action has been massively expanded as a result of the Government's investments in area-based action. These rapidly growing activities, or 'early hits' as politicians are sometimes wont to call them, are significant short-term achievements, therefore; but evaluation of the longer-term outcomes of area-based action is also critical in assessing its impact in combating the more general problems of poverty and social exclusion.

Such evaluation will flow from the independent research which the Government has commissioned to assess more broadly the achievements (and the failures) of the ABIs. There are major evaluation projects associated with all of the larger ABI programmes, but, as most programmes themselves are scheduled to run for between four and seven years, it will take time to process findings and reach conclusions. One of the early assessments that almost all evaluators share, however, is the conclusion that area-based action will in itself take time to produce meaningful and sustainable changes in patterns of local poverty and deprivation, and that critical to the achievement of such longer-term change will be the processes of articulation and organisation that form the basis for local action – in short, changing outcomes will require changing processes too.

This is recognised in the commitments within all ABI programmes to the promotion of partnership working and participation as key elements in the delivery of local policy practice. Partnership is a key theme underlying new developments across public service provision in Britain. For instance, Sullivan and Skelcher list over fifty multi-agency partnerships operating in 2001/02,[11] and point out that it is at local level where the greatest 'congestion' of initiatives is felt.[12] There is a clear expectation that partnership bodies will be established to provide strategic direction for activities within area-based programmes, most notably in the establishment of local strategic partnerships (LSPs) in all of the 88 local authority districts in receipt of NRF support.[13]

Participation of local residents and communities is also at the forefront of policy implementation. Early evaluation of the NDCs stressed the importance of including residents and community groups,[14] and the guidance on LSPs pointed out that 'attention should be given at an early stage to ensuring that all sections of the community have the opportunity to participate'.[15] Participation also extends into expectations of the way all levels of government, including local authorities, should now be (re)engaging with their constituencies.[16]

Partnership and participation are critically important to the achievement of longer-term changes in the extent of deprivation and exclusion within poor neighbourhoods and districts. Indeed, such *procedural inclusion* is as significant in challenging and changing longstanding experiences of local deprivation as are the substantive changes to policy delivery and practice that may flow from this. Establishing a constructive engagement between those involved in delivering local services and those (potentially) receiving them can help to ensure that locally experienced needs can be identified and available resources (re)directed to addressing these. Procedural inclusion can change the way policy is planned therefore; but there is more to it than this.

Partnership and participation are also to some extent themselves both goals and achievements. Through challenging agency boundaries and practices and through including individuals and communities in policy planning, real shifts in the use and distribution of power and resources will necessarily take place and will bring those marginalised from those social institutions into a more central role within their local communities. The broader concept of social exclusion recognises, as we discussed, those dimensions of deprivation that extend beyond control over financial resources to include also problems of alienation and marginalisation from local services. Reform of public services and empowerment of local communities and citizens in themselves can operate to combat some of these forms of exclusion. Changing *how* we do things is an achievement in itself.

## The limitations of area-based action

Whatever the achievements of recent (and past) area-based anti-poverty action, however, it is essential to recognise the important, indeed the fundamental, limitations within the area-based approach to policy practice. For a start, we must not forget the intrinsic limitation of spatial targeting of policy action. This has sometimes in the past been referred to as the 'ecological fallacy' – many poor people do live in poor areas, but so too do many non-poor people, and (more significantly) many poor people live outside of them. Evidence to the House of Commons Select Committee on Work and Pensions argued that two-thirds of poor families did not live in the poor areas targeted by ABI programmes, although data from the Index of Multiple Deprivation suggests that 54 per cent of poor children do live in the 20 per cent most deprived wards.[17] Targeting activity onto poor areas will not guarantee that all poverty (and exclusion) can be addressed.

This conundrum has been explored more recently by Powell and others, who develop a more sophisticated distinction between 'people poverty', which cannot directly be addressed by area-based policy action, and 'place poverty', which potentially can.[18] The issue has also been taken up by Lupton, working at the Centre for the Analysis of Social Exclusion (CASE) at the London School of Economics. There are two important dimensions to Lupton's analysis.

First, she points out that the identification and measurement of the spatial dimension of poverty is, in practice, considerably more complex than some policy makers and critics sometimes think. In England, the identification of areas of deprivation, and the allocation of funding for programmes, such as neighbourhood renewal, has drawn heavily on the new Index of Deprivation, developed for the Government.[19] This employs a wider range of measures than previous indices of deprivation and focuses upon the incomes and circumstances of local residents. It is certainly a better way of identifying the spatial distribution of poverty than some earlier measures, and is particularly effective in targeting the urban poor, the unemployed and poor children; for activities which seek to address the needs of such groups, it may be an effective method of targeting. Inevitably, however, it has its limitations (for instance, in identifying rural poverty) and, as Lupton points out, the more general concern is to ensure that appropriate measures are used for specific forms of initiative.[20] Targeting needs to be sophisticated.

Second, she takes up the question of the extent to which we can accurately measure the impact of policy action within local areas. This is, in part, a question of the appropriate mix of quantitative and qualitative methodologies, which there is not the space to explore here. It is also, however, about the problems of understanding and attributing the processes of social change. For instance, how can we distinguish between the dimensions of people and place poverty? How do we measure a moving target and take account of the mobility within and between neighbourhoods? How do we separate neighbourhood initiatives and neighbourhood effects from the broader social process within which local change takes place?[21] Neighbourhoods, and other local areas, are neither static nor socially discrete.

These practical limitations within the area-based policy approach, however, are also linked to some difficult problems of principle which lie behind the effectiveness, and the desirability, of local policy action. The fact that local areas are neither static nor discrete exposes a contradiction which lies at the heart of area-based policy action. This is the implicit assumption that problems of poverty and exclusion experienced locally are (to some extent at least) caused locally, and therefore can be solved locally. And this assumption can lead to a *pathologisation* of local poverty and anti-poverty action.

The model of partnership and participation means that local citizens and communities are encouraged to participate in the programmes designed to improve local services and regenerate their local areas because this will ensure that future provision reflects local needs. At the same time, this process of involvement will make local people active agents in their own social improvement leading to further empowerment. Whatever the practical difficulties in this, the empowerment of local agents appears to be an unqualified good.

However, the expectation that local citizens can be, and should be, the agents of local regeneration suggests that this is so because it is they who are the authors of their current misfortunes. The danger in this is that of the classic case of 'blaming the victim'. It is a concern that has consistently been voiced by critics of earlier area-based anti-poverty action, most notably one of the first examples, the ' War on Poverty' of the 1960s. Writing about the US experience in a book entitled *Blaming the Victim* in 1971, Ryan argued that social problems were being identified as being associated with the circumstances of those experiencing them and then policy makers were constructing 'humanitarian action programmes' to get people to correct these themselves.[22] At best, this was therefore a case of 'helping the poor to help themselves' – a slogan widely used within the US 'War on Poverty' lexicon of the time. At worst, it was pathologising local poverty.

It is unlikely that the British politicians and policy makers of the new century would subscribe to such an overtly pathological model of social improvement. However, in a more covert form it is an ever-present danger in the area-based approach to anti-poverty policy. In particular, for instance, the insistence on local solutions to local problems can suggest that all such problems and solutions are locally based. In the case of broader economic forces (such as those leading to the closure of local employers) or of broader public service shortcomings (such as lack of health or social care places) this is clearly not so. And achieving change in private industrial investment or public spending on health and social care is not a solution which is open to local agents, no matter how actively they participate in local partnerships and projects.

## Conclusion

Writing about the American War on Poverty over thirty years ago, Clark and Hopkins concluded that,

> ...deprivation in many areas...may not be responsive to programmes of amelioration and community action. The problems of poverty cannot be resolved as if they were isolated from the wider economic, social and political patterns of the nation.[23]

This is a conclusion which remains relevant to the area-based programmes in Britain at the beginning of the new century. The arguments for targeting resources (and policy action) onto areas where levels of poverty are highest and for involving local citizens in determining and delivering local solutions to the problems of poverty and exclusion that blight their neighbourhoods, should not blind us to the inevitable limitations of such local action.

Many decisions affecting the circumstances and the services in local areas are taken elsewhere, and local participation and partnership may not be able to influence these, no matter how effective and committed. More pertinently perhaps, a concentration on local action may lead other national (and international) decision makers to conclude that they need not remain responsible for, and attentive to, such local manifestations of inequality and deprivation – these are being tackled by local action.

The biggest danger here is that area-based activity therefore deflects concern, and policy development, away from the broader contexts and processes within which local poverty and exclusion, however concentrated, is constructed and maintained. Or worse still, that it provides a convenient reason for not tackling these potentially more difficult forces. Area-based action must not become an excuse for inaction elsewhere.

It would not be fair to suggest, however, that such tokenism is either the intention or the effect of recent government policy in the UK. There is much evidence that the Labour Government does understand the broader economic and social forces which contribute to the problems of poverty and social exclusion that it has rightly pledged to combat, as the other contributions to this volume confirm. Nor would it be right to dismiss the very real achievements of local action (and local activists) in bringing about much-needed improvements in their local neighbourhoods, and in raising local participation and empowerment in so doing. Area-based programmes are making a difference and things are getting better in some of the most deprived areas.

However, it is important too to remember that there are limitations to the goals and the achievements of local anti-poverty action. The growth in our concern about and understanding of the spatial distribution of poverty means that we do now know much more about the uneven geographical spread of deprivation and this has led policy makers to target policy action onto those areas where levels of poverty are highest. However, we cannot expect local action to combat national (or international) social forces. Local action can only achieve so much local change; it must be accompanied by other action at other points in social and economic structures – and it is essential that both national and local policy makers understand this. We should all know our limitations. At the beginning of this chapter we posed the question: why does it matter where people are poor? It matters, only if we remember that this is not why they are poor.

## Notes

1 C Philo (ed), *Off the Map: the social geography of poverty in the UK*, Child Poverty Action Group, 1995

2 D Herbert and D Smith, *Social Problems and the City: geographical perspectives*, Oxford University Press, 1979

3 See note 2 for an early example; and more recently J Hills, J Le Grand and D Piachaud (eds), *Understanding Social Exclusion*, Oxford University Press, 2002 and R Lupton, *Poverty Street: the dynamics of neighbourhood decline and renewal*, The Policy Press, 2003

4 Performance and Innovation Unit, *The Role of Central Government at Regional and Local Level*, Cabinet Office, 2000

5 Regional Co-ordination Unit, *Review of Area-Based Initiatives: action plans*, Office of the Deputy Prime Minister, 2002

6 See G Room (ed), *Beyond the Threshold: the measurement and analysis of social exclusion*, The Policy Press, 1995 and J Hills, J Le Grand and D Piachaud (eds), *Understanding Social Exclusion*, Oxford University Press, 2002

7 Department for Work and Pensions, *Opportunity for All: fourth annual report*, DWP, 2002

8 See the SEU website at www.socialexclusionunit.gov.uk

9 Social Exclusion Unit, *Bringing Britain together: a national strategy for neighbourhood renewal*, The Stationery Office, 1998; Social Exclusion Unit, *National Strategy for Neighbourhood Renewal: a framework for consultation*, The Stationery Office, 2000; Social Exclusion Unit, *A New Commitment to Neighbourhood Renewal: national strategy action plan*, The Stationery Office, 2001

10 See Regional Co-ordination Unit, *Area-based Initiative: case studies*, Office of the Deputy Prime Minister, 2003

11 H Sullivan and C Skelcher, *Working across Boundaries: collaboration in public services*, Palgrave, 2002, pp228-37

12 See note 10, p225

13 Department of Environment, Transport and the Regions, *Local Strategic Partnerships: consultation document*, DETR, 2000

14 Department of Environment, Transport and the Regions, *Learning Lessons: Pathfinders*, 1999, p7

15 See note 13, para 2.20

16 V Lowndes, L Pratchett and G Stoker, 'Trends in Public Participation: Parts 1 and 2', *Public Administration*, 79:1 and 2, 2001, pp205-22 and 445-55

17 Select Committee on Work and Pensions, *Fifth Report: Childcare for Working Parents*, House of Commons, 2003

18 M Powell, R Boyne and R Ashworth R, 'Towards a Geography of People Poverty and Place Poverty', *Policy and Politics*, 29:3, 2002, pp243-58

19 Department of Environment, Transport and the Regions, *Indices of Deprivation 2000*, DETR, 2000

20 R Tunstall and R Lupton, 'Is Targeting Deprived Areas an Effective Means to Reach Poor People? An assessment of one rationale for area-based funding programmes', CASEpaper 70, London School of Economics, 2003

21 R Lupton, 'Neighbourhood Effects: can we measure them and does it matter?', CASEpaper 73, London School of Economics, 2003

22 W Ryan, *Blaming the Victim*, Orbach and Chambers, 1971, p8

23 K Clark and J Hopkins, *A Relevant War Against Poverty: a study of community action programmes and observable social change*, Harper and Row, 1968, p256

# Three

# 'Vulnerability' and child poverty: *Every Child Matters*

*Neera Sharma*

## Introduction

The Government has introduced a range of policies as part of its commitment to end child poverty by 2020. The *Households Below Average Income* report shows that child poverty has been reduced by 500,000 since 1997.[1] However, independent research has suggested that following the Government's initial reforms, some of the poorest children, approximately 300,000 or nearly one in six children, had become worse off.[2] This research predates the tax credit spending which has improved the lives of many children (see Chapters Five and Seven), but it demonstrates that not all change has been in a positive direction. A recent report from Save the Children highlights the fact that there are one million children who are living in severe and persistent poverty.[3] This indicates that, although it may be easier to lift those children who are just below the poverty line above it, it will be potentially more difficult to lift the most vulnerable children out of poverty.

The Government has not published a co-ordinated strategy which demonstrates how *all* children, including the most disadvantaged and vulnerable, will be lifted out of poverty. Such a strategy is not captured in either *Opportunity for All* or the UK National Action Plan on Social Inclusion. The Government's response to Lord Laming's enquiry into the death of eight-year-old Victoria Climbié, the Green Paper *Every Child Matters*, provided the context for setting out such a strategy, set as it is within the broader context of the Government's existing social policy programme. In his speech on the Green Paper at Toynbee Hall, the Chief Secretary to the Treasury, Paul Boateng MP, said:

> And, we don't just want to tackle child poverty. We also want to develop modern policies that provide opportunity and fulfilment. We want to both protect children and maximise their potential

Regrettably, the rhetoric does not match the reality: the Green Paper provided an unprecedented opportunity to improve the lives and opportunities of the most vulnerable and disadvantaged children. Although it is set within the overall context of the Government's pledge to end child poverty, it does not address how this part of its agenda will be taken forward.

This chapter sets out the main proposals in *Every Child Matters* and argues that the needs of specific groups of vulnerable children are not addressed. These include disabled children, asylum-seeking and refugee children, children in homeless families, and Black and ethnic minority children. As we were going to press the Children Bill 2004 was published. The main clauses in the Bill are generally reflective of the proposals set out in the Green Paper and the main thrust of this chapter is, therefore, unaffected.

## The Green Paper: an outline of the key proposals

The policies and proposals set out in the Green Paper are designed to protect children and maximise their potential. In setting out a framework for services that cover children and young people from birth to 19 living in England, it aims to reduce the numbers of children who experience educational failure, engage in offending or anti-social behaviour, suffer from ill-health, or become teenage parents or victims of abuse and neglect.

The Green Paper's proposals take into account the results of the Children's and Young People's Unit consultation which revealed that the five outcomes that mattered most to children and young people included economic well-being, as well as health, safety, developing the skills needed for adulthood and participation in their communities. The key concern expressed by young people, that they should not be prevented by economic disadvantage from achieving their full potential in life, is not addressed by the Green Paper.

The Green Paper focuses on four main areas:

- **Supporting parents and carers:** with a £25m Parenting Fund to be spent on improving universal services, such as schools, and health and social services.
- **Early intervention and effective protection:** through measures such as improving information sharing; ensuring that there is one lead pro-

fessional working with a child; a common assessment framework and ensuring that services are delivered in multi-disciplinary teams based in schools and children's centres.

- **Accountability and integration – locally, regionally and nationally:** through the creation of Directors of Children's Services responsible for education and social services; integrating key services in children's trusts by 2006; establishing local children's safeguarding boards; and creating the post of a Children's Commissioner.
- **Workforce reform:** by establishing a Children's Workforce Unit in the Department for Education and Skills and a Sector Skills Council for Children and Young People's Services.

The key policy areas for improving outcomes for children are Sure Start, raising school standards and eradicating child poverty. The Government wishes to build on these by:

- creating Sure Start children's centres in each of the 20 per cent most deprived neighbourhoods;
- promoting full service-extended schools, which are open beyond school hours to provide breakfast and after-school clubs, and child-care;
- increasing the focus on activities for children out of school through the creation of a Young People's Fund with an initial budget of £200 million;
- tackling homelessness;
- reforms to the youth justice system;
- investing in child and adolescent mental health services.

## The exclusion of vulnerable children and the lack of an overarching framework

The Green Paper does not address the needs of the most vulnerable children. The lack of an overarching framework underpinned by the United Nations (UN) Convention on the Rights of the Child and incorporating basic principles regarding the welfare of children is a serious shortcoming. This results in a situation where its title cannot be justified. The Paper's proposals, if fully implemented, will not demonstrate that *every* child matters.

Exemptions in the Green Paper and related documents, the continued separation of some aspects of services to children through current structures of government and other legislative proposals affect children in trouble, those who are refugees and asylum seekers, some children in homeless families and disabled children.

If some children are excluded from services they will become vulnerable. Policies that provide care and safety and are inclusive of all children are essential to prevent some children 'slipping through the system'.

## Disabled children

### Introduction

Disabled children number around 320,000 ,just 3 per cent of the child population, but are especailly vulnerable to poverty and disadvantage throughout their childhoods and into adulthood. Over 55 per cent of families with disabled children experience poverty at some time in their lives.[5] The Government's strategy of work as a route out of poverty, supported by the National Childcare Strategy, has not so far had the same poverty-reducing impact on families with disabled children as it has had on other families.[6] The Green Paper misses the opportunity to address this.

The reasons why disabled children are most vulnerable to poverty and social exclusion are well researched and if disabled children matter, then their needs should have been closely linked into the proposed new structures and processes. There are a number of examples of how the linkages between poverty and a strategy to tackle these could have been incorporated into the Green Paper.

### Work and poverty

Parents with disabled children are often unable to work because they cannot secure childcare suitable for their child's needs. Just 3 per cent of mothers with a disabled child work full time compared with 22 per cent of mothers with non-disabled children.[7] Furthermore, community-based leisure facilities are rarely available for families with disabled children

However, the Green Paper does not make a commitment to any additional funding or targets to ensure that the Sure Start children's centres or day care services can meet the needs of disabled children. Furthermore, many poor children, including disabled children, live outside the deprived areas targeted for help by the government initiatives and so will miss out.

Enabling parents of disabled children to find and stay in employment requires appropriate holiday and after-school provision, as well as appropriate day care. The proposals in the Green Paper for after-school clubs and extended schools do not demonstrate how disabled children and young people will be included. In addition to extra funding, ensuring inclusion demands integrating a number of services, especially transport. The Green Paper stresses the importance of integrating key services, but omits to recognise the importance of transport. This is crucial if disabled children are to be given the opportunity to participate in community life.

The provision of day care and community-based leisure facilities requires the training of appropriate specialist staff, including childminders. Specialist day care for disabled children is difficult to find and many services for children under eight fail to provide for disabled children at all. The review of workforce and training in the Green Paper required a focus specifically on the training needs and pay of staff who can meet the needs of disabled children.

## Additional expenditure

Families with disabled children incur ongoing additional expenditure. It costs, on average, three times as much to raise a child with a severe impairment as a non-disabled child.[8] At present, benefits do not meet these needs.[9] Furthermore, many parents are confused about entitlements to benefits and find procedures overly complicated.[10] As a result, take-up is limited and the poorest families are not accessing the benefits they need.[11]

Although the Green Paper is set within the context of tackling poverty there is no recognition of the extra costs of caring for a disabled child and how this should be addressed within a framework of financial support which directly benefits the most vulnerable children.

## Educational outcomes

Disabled children are more likely than their non-disabled peers to leave school without qualifications.[12] Seventy per cent of disabled adults rely wholly on benefits for income and have low expectations of employment.

The proposals relating to education and extended schools in the Green Paper do not include the needs of disabled children and their families. It is imperative that extended schools are developed as inclusive, and that both mainstream and extended schools are included in planning services.

## Supporting parents

The Green Paper builds on a strategy for supporting parents, which is backed by additional funding. However, there is no recognition that the parents of disabled children have additional support and training needs to enable them to take part in general parent support programmes.

The co-ordination of services through improved inter-agency working, for example, children's trusts, has the potential to ease the lives of parents of disabled children, who are frequently in touch with several agencies. This could also include advice about services, employment, training and access to benefits. The Green Paper does not explore how children's trusts could meet the needs of disabled children and their families.

## Supporting the most vulnerable disabled children and young people

It is well evidenced that disabled children from ethnic minority communities face additional disadvantage and social exclusion.[14] The Green Paper makes no reference to the needs of this comparatively small, but most vulnerable and excluded, group of children.

In summing up this section, it is evident that the Green Paper does not address how its proposals will break the unacceptable cycle of poverty and deprivation of disabled children and their families.

## Asylum-seeking children

Asylum-seeking and refugee children represent a vulnerable group within society. There are a number of major concerns among statutory and voluntary organisations working with asylum-seeking children; concerns which are not addressed by the Green Paper and which will result in the continuing impoverishment and social exclusion of these children.

## Poverty

Children are living in families who have no entitlement to welfare benefits. Support from the National Asylum Support Service (NASS) is very basic and 30 per cent live below the poverty line.[15] A joint study by Oxfam and the Refugee Council showed that 85 per cent experience hunger, 95 per cent cannot afford to buy clothes or shoes and 80 per cent are not able to maintain good health.[16] The report reveals that many asylum seekers do not receive the basic support to which they may be entitled, due to an inefficient system.

The links between poverty and poor adult outcomes are well researched: the children and young people consulted when the Green Paper was drafted cited economic well-being as a key determinant in achieving their potential. The Green Paper was an opportunity to make recommendations to bring to an end a system which ensures that children in asylum-seeking and refugee families are growing up well below the poverty line, impacting on their lives as children now and into adulthood.

## Social exclusion

There are also serious issues concerning the dispersal system, whereby those seeking accommodation can be moved anywhere in the country by NASS. The experience of dispersal results in children being isolated from their own community, language and religion. They are often moved to areas where they feel alienated and isolated.[17]

It is difficult to see how the proposals in the Green Paper will touch the lives of these children when they are such a transient population. This would require an end to the dispersal system so that families have the opportunity to become part of a community, supported by local agencies, such as schools. It would also require sufficient flexibility and targeted funding within the new structures, especially extended schools and children's centres, to ensure that they reach and include this vulnerable group of children and families.

## Delivering services

The lack of information concerning how many children are living in asylum-seeking and refugee families makes it difficult to plan services. Although

NASS provides local education authorities with the details of school-age children moving into their area, it cannot tell whether these children will actually arrive or remain for a sufficient time to need a school place. Furthermore, many unaccompanied children, and indeed children with families, often 'disappear' from the system in much the same way as children in the care system once disappeared.[18]

Once again, the Green Paper is silent on how these children will be protected through improved sharing of information and through the proposed common assessment framework, or how lead professions will take responsibility to ensure that these children receive the services they require.

Asylum-seeking children should matter as much as any other children, yet the existing legislation cuts off some of them from the services and protections available to other children. New legislation promises, for the first time, to make it possible for some families with children to have no right to accommodation or any form of support, and to maintain the current prohibition on asylum seekers working. Some children will be pushed to the margins of society, without the safety nets that protect all other children.

## Children in homeless families

The statistics on children in homeless families are alarming.

- 750,000 families with children live in poor housing.[19]
- 100,000 children were homeless in 2001.[20]
- Over 300,000 families with children live in overcrowded housing.[21]
- 81,250 homeless households, many of them families with children, are in temporary acccommodation – a rise of 86 per cent since 1997.[22]
- 6,700 families with children are living in bed and breakfast accomodation.[23]

Homeless families live transient lives, which cut them off from support networks, both formal and informal. They have difficulty accessing schools, social services support, nurseries and GPs, as well as being cut off from extended families and other community support.

The Green Paper recognises the links between childhood poverty and homelessness. However, it does not ensure that tackling homelessness is an integral part of the new structures and processes. The links between homelessness and support systems, such as housing benefit, are not made.

The Green Paper states that by March 2004 no homeless family with children should be placed in bed and breakfast accommodation, except in an emergency. This claim is spurious. No family who has been placed in bed and breakfast accommodation by social services departments or by NASS is classed as homeless and no accommodation which is owned or managed by a statutory or voluntary body is classed as bed and breakfast accommodation, even if it is identical in nature or of worse quality than that which is classed as bed and breakfast. Families living in this accommodation are thus excluded from this pledge.

Children in all homeless families are vulnerable and in need of services. They should all be included in the pledge to reduce the numbers of children living in bed and breakfast accommodation.

There are numerous examples of how the Green Paper could have ensured that children in homeless families would be specifically targeted.

- The cycle of benefits and temporary accommodation must be broken. Homeless families in temporary accommodation and the private rented sector are in a poverty trap. Housing benefit impacts on wider issues and needs to be addressed.
- Children's trusts (or similar structures) need to work effectively with other agencies to support homeless families with children, especially those at risk.
- There is a need for services, both regionally and nationally, to reach out to socially excluded groups, such as travellers and asylum seekers.
- Children's centres and Sure Start operate on an area basis and do not necessarily cover temporary accommodation. Services should reach out beyond these boundaries and children in temporary accommodation should be given priority for childcare services.

## Black and ethnic minority children

Research shows that whilst there is much variation between different ethnic groups, a child born into an ethnic minority household is likely to suffer poverty and disadvantage. In particular, s/he:

- is more likely to be born into a poor household, especially if Pakistani or Bangladeshi;[24]
- is more likely to be part of a large family, especially if Asian;[25]
- may have less access to public services than a White child, while also having cultural and religious requirements which mainstream provision may not cater for;[26]
- is less likely to achieve well in school especially if male and Black Caribbean.[27]

It is evident that ethnic minorities, especially children, are disproportionately worse off than the population as a whole. Research from Save the Children suggests that a quarter of children in severe poverty are of non-White ethnicity.[28] Unemployment rates for ethnic minority males are up to three times higher than those for Whites, with high rates for Bangladeshis and Black Africans.[29]

Initiatives which build on existing provision will need to be developed in a way that meet the needs of Black and ethnic minority children and provide levers to break the cycle of poverty and social exclusion. The Green Paper does not address specifically the needs of these children. There are several key areas in which the development of policy and the delivery of services need to be attuned to their needs.

## Education

The Department for Education and Skills has published a strategy paper called *Aiming High* to raise ethnic minority achievement. The Green Paper does not explore how the proposed structures will progress the proposals set out in the strategy paper. For example, how will the additional funding in schools be allocated so that it reaches those most in need? Extended schools could exclude those children who are already disaffected with the educational system.  How will parental support be offered to those parents for whom English is not a first language?

## Barriers to employment

Black and ethnic minority young people and adults face barriers in securing employment or training and are disproportionately represented in low-paid jobs. For example, despite performing better than Whites in terms of education, Indians still have a lower employment rate.[30] The role of extended schools, and particularly Connexions, in tackling barriers to employment and training for young people from Black and ethnic minority communities will be crucial in ensuring that future generations of young people are able to secure the employment to lift them out of poverty. The Green Paper misses the opportunity to define the role of agencies in addressing the employment and training needs of Black and ethnic minority children.

## Childcare

The National Childcare Strategy is a key driver in the Government's strategy to end poverty. Use of formal childcare is lower among ethnic minority groups: only 79 per cent of Black parents and 68 per cent of Asian parents use childcare compared with 87 per cent of White.[31] Nearly all children of White parents have recently attended a nursery provider compared with 88 per cent of ethnic minority children of the same age.[32]

Meeting the childcare needs of Black and ethnic minority parents requires a well-resourced and targeted strategy which makes available sufficient places across the age range and provides childcare which is affordable, accessible and responsive to the needs of Black and ethnic minority parents. The focus on deprived areas within the National Childcare Strategy misses many parents who live outside the areas targeted for help.

## Barriers to services

Although there are many examples of good practice, there is evidence that the ethnic minority population has less confidence in some services than their White counterparts. For example, social care services may not easily be accessed by ethnic minority communities or may not be appropriate to their needs. For a number of reasons, certain ethnic minority groups are harder to reach using mainstream services than others.

The Green Paper aims to make services more accessible and integrated, with lead professionals ensuring that children do not slip through the net. However, the specific needs of Black and ethnic minority children and their families are not addressed.

## Other vulnerable groups

There are also other vulnerable groups of children for whom breaking the cycle of poverty and disadvantage is critical if the Government is to meet its pledge to end child poverty. These include children in trouble and children in traveller families. Again, the Green Paper lacks a focus on the needs of these children, especially children in travelling families.

Although the Green Paper discusses the needs of young people and creates a Young People's Fund with an initial budget of £200 million, there is a disturbing disjuncture in the tone and effect of the Green Paper and the paper, *Youth Justice Next Steps*. This disjuncture is also apparent in the effect of the Anti-Social Behaviour Bill. The lack of coherence and shared principles can be seen most explicitly in a youth justice system that remains indistinct from the adult criminal justice system and which is not committed to compliance with the UN Convention on the Rights of the Child. This militates against the attention to welfare concerns set out in the Green Paper.

Key services for children should be integrated at both local and national level: the Green Paper is clear on that. However, the separation of responsibility for policy for disabled children (Department of Health) and children in trouble (Home Office) from that for other children (Department for Education and Skills) threatens integration at national level.

## Conclusion

There is a missed opportunity within the Green Paper, subsequently reflected in the Children Bill, to ensure that new structures and processes specifically include the most vulnerable children and young people in our society. This needs to start with a commitment to the UN Convention on the Rights of the Child and the development of a set of overarching principles, which include a focus on vulnerable groups of children. This must be matched by government structures that deliver services in a co-ordinated way to all children.

At present, there is a lack of clarity as to who at a local level is responsible for monitoring and reporting on child poverty. Such a responsibility needs to be part of the role of the new Directors of Children's Services. This would encompass collating information, and monitoring and reporting on the progress made on child poverty.

The success of key initiatives depends on effective co-ordination and the ability to make interventions appropriately. So, for example, if children do not make use of extended schools because of lack of transport or the money for the fare home, or are prevented from participation in activities because of lack of money this needs to be addressed. It is appropriate that the Directors of Children's Services discharge this responsibility.

The Government's anti-poverty strategy is based on the supposition that policies which are not specifically targeted, such as welfare to work, will take all children out of poverty. However, such policies will take the least poorest children out of poverty. It is difficult to see how those children who are severely and persistently poor, for example disabled children, will be taken out of poverty without specific and targeted measures.

In a similar vein, the Green Paper is built on the premise that universal services, with some targeting, will reach all. If 'every child matters' then it is imperative that the changes to children's services that follow on from the Green Paper take place alongside a co-ordinated and resourced strategy that includes the most vulnerable groups of children. It is only in this way that we can start to ensure that every child matters and that all children can be lifted out of poverty.

## Notes

1 Department for Work and Pensions, *Households Below Average Incomes, 1994/95-2001/02*, Corporate Document Services, 2003

2 H Sunderland, *Five Labour Budgets (1997-2001): impacts on the distribution of household incomes and on child poverty*, Microsimulation Unit Research Note 41, May 2001

3 L Adelman, S Middleton and K Ashworth, *Britain's Poorest Children: severe and persistent poverty and social exclusion*, Centre for Research in Social Policy and Save the Children, 2003

4 Office of Population and Census Surveys, *The Prevalence of Disability Amongst Children*, Volume 3, Corporate Document Services, 1989

5 D Gordon and R Parker, *Disabled Children in Britain: a re-analysis of the OPCS Disability Survey*, The Stationery Office, 2000

6 N Sharma, *Still Missing Out? Ending poverty and social exclusion: messages to government from families with disabled children*, Barnardo's, 2002

7 *Patterns of Employment in Mothers with and without Disabled Children*, Family Fund Trust, 2002; and *General Household Survey 2002*, as quoted in *Disabled Children, Their Families and Child Poverty*, Briefing Paper, Council for Disabled Children and End Child Poverty, 2003

8 B Dobson and S Middleton, *Paying to Care: the cost of childhood disability*, Joseph Rowntree Foundation, York, 1998

9 See note 8

10 see note 8

11 L Reith, 'Children, Poverty and Disability', *Poverty 109*, Child Poverty Action Group, 2001, pp10-13

12 Disability Rights Commission, *Educating for Equality*, Disability Rights Commission, 2002

13 Disability Rights Commission, *Mori Poll Survey of the Views of Young Disabled People*, Disability Rights Commission, 2002

14 Department of Health, *Valuing People: a national strategy for people with learning disabilities*, Corporate Document Services, 2001

15 Refugee Council information www.refugeecouncil.org.uk, 2002

16 See note 15

17 The Children's Legal Centre, *Mapping the Provision of Education and Social Services for Refugee and Asylum-seeker Children: lessons from the eastern region*, Children's Legal Centre, 2003

18 See note 17

19 Department of the Environment, Transport and the Regions, *English Housing Condition Survey*, Corporate Document Services, 1996

20 Estimated by Shelter (2001) and quoted in *Child Poverty, Housing and Homelessness*, Joint briefing paper, Shelter and End Child Poverty, 2003

21 See note 19

22 Office for the Deputy Prime Minister, *Statutory Homelessness Bulletin*, September 2002, quoted in note 20

23 See note 23

24 Department for Work and Pensions, *Opportunity for All*, Corporate Document Services, 2003

25 See note 24

26 See note 24

27 Department for Education and Skills, *Aiming High: raising the achievement of ethnic minority pupils*, Corporate Document Services, 2003

28 See note 3

29 Department for Work and Pensions, *Ethnic Minorities and the Labour Market*, 2003

30 See note 24

31 Strategy Unit, *Ethnic Minorities and the Labour Market*, 2003

32 Department for Education and Skills, *ethnic minority Attainment and Participation in Education and Training*, 2002

# Four

# Childcare and child poverty

*Lisa Harker*

Despite growing interest in the contribution childcare can make to the Government's anti-poverty agenda, the UK remains about thirty years behind some of its European neighbours in terms of the level of state investment in provision. There is one childcare place for every five children under the age of eight and access to a place is still largely determined by parents' ability to pay. This chapter considers the contribution that childcare has made to reducing child poverty and where policy needs to go next if the UK is to achieve among the lowest child poverty rates in Europe.

## Childcare and the anti-poverty agenda

Early years services have long played a role in tackling poverty and social exclusion. From the beginning of the twentieth century the provision of free pre-school education was viewed as a means of enhancing attainment and promoting well-being among children living in disadvantaged circumstances. After the Second World War, publicly funded daycare services for younger children were allocated for the most disadvantaged. The importance of childcare to the poorest children has, therefore, long been recognised. But despite this, childcare has largely remained a private matter. Most provision, other than pre-school education, has not relied on public subsidy, but rather on parental contributions.

Until the late 1990s childcare was not viewed as a serious political issue. This changed with the election of a Labour government and its focus on 'welfare to work'. The success of one of the Government's flagship policies – the New Deal – was very dependent on the availability of childcare and for the first time childcare began to be seen as an issue of major political importance. In his first Budget speech in July 1997 Gordon Brown left us in no doubt of the Government's commitment to childcare:

> Childcare will no longer be seen as an afterthought or a fringe element of social policies but from now on – as it should be – an integral part of our economic policy.

The welfare to work focus has meant childcare for working parents has been a priority, but this has been part of a strategy to reduce poverty and social exclusion by increasing the chance of parents taking paid work. The lack of affordable childcare for low-income families has become an increasing concern; the high cost of childcare provision means that families on low incomes are those least likely to have access to a childcare place.

The introduction of the childcare tax credit in 1999 (replacing the childcare disregard) aimed to reduce the cost of childcare for parents on a low income. Low-income families can receive help with up to 70 per cent of their childcare costs, up to a maximum level. There has also been increased investment in out-of-school childcare provision to ease the difficulty of combining paid work with caring for school-age children. A five-year New Opportunities Fund programme was launched in 1998 to increase the level of out-of school-provision, with a particular focus on creating services to increase employment in deprived areas.

As the private childcare market sector has expanded, the Government has also tried to address market failure in the childcare system. Under the National Childcare Strategy, introduced in 1998, the Government has established a delivery infrastructure through which to monitor the demand and supply of childcare provision (early years development and childcare partnerships).[1] Pump-prime funding has been directed towards developing services, particularly in disadvantaged areas where services struggle to be sustainable. The neighbourhood nurseries initiative, for example, was launched in 2000 in order to create 45,000 new childcare places in the most disadvantaged areas.

There has also been growing recognition within government of the value of good-quality childcare for the development of children, especially those living in disadvantaged circumstances. This has meant that childcare is increasingly seen not only as a service that enables parents to work, thereby reducing family poverty, but also as a valuable means of providing a beneficial environment for children. Childcare policy has been influenced by studies, mostly undertaken in the United States, that have found links between children's early years experience and later behavioural and academic achievement.

Over a hundred centres have been designated 'early excellence centres' since 1997 because they offer high-quality provision that combines early education and daycare services, parenting support, special educational needs, access to adult education and training, health and other community services. Although they work with children from all backgrounds, the centres are strongly focused on promoting social inclusion for isolated and disadvantaged families.

Evidence of the value of early years' services for children's development was also particularly influential in persuading the Government to introduce the Sure Start programme in 1998, integrating daycare, health and parenting services at a local level. The programme provides services and support for all children under the age of four and their parents in targeted areas of deprivation, with specific aims to reduce various aspects of social exclusion.[2] Now operating in over 500 areas, the programme is reaching 400,000 children, one in three children living in poverty.

Recognition of the importance of good-quality early years services to children's development has continued to shape policy development. Concern about the childcare needs of the poorest children was a major theme underlying the recommendations of the 2002 inter-departmental childcare review[3] and has underpinned the recent review of childcare conducted as part of the Government's 2004 Spending Review. The Government now plans to develop 'children's centres', offering integrated early education and full daycare, health services, and family and parenting support, firstly in the 20 per cent most disadvantaged wards in England by 2006, but ultimately in every community.[4]

## Recent improvements

Although still very low by European standards, access to childcare services has improved in recent years. There is now one childcare place for every five children under the age of eight[5] and nearly all three- and four-year-olds have access to a part-time pre-school education place. Although provision is still limited, there has been a substantial increase in out-of-school services; over 500,000 new places have been created in the UK since 1997.[6]

It is likely that this increase in childcare services has contributed towards tackling poverty and social exclusion in two ways: both by helping parents take up employment (thereby increasing family income and opportunities), and by providing children with the social, emotional and cognitive stimulation that is beneficial for their development.

More than half of lone parents are now in work compared with 44 per cent in 1997[7] and since 1997 the percentage of children living in work-less households has fallen from 17.9 per cent to 15.2 per cent.[8] Additional childcare provision is perceived to have contributed to these trends.

Although few doubt the valuable contribution childcare can make in enabling parents to take up paid employment, it is rarely possible to isolate the impact of childcare provision on employment patterns. The absence of childcare is frequently identified by parents as a barrier to work and (it is assumed) higher income, but the provision of childcare is rarely associated with a direct increase in employment. It is not, perhaps, surprising that the picture is a complicated one: parents' decisions to work are complex and shaped by personal beliefs about work and parenthood.

It is even more challenging to isolate, as yet, the impact of increased childcare provision on children's enhanced development. There is, of course, already a substantial body of research that shows that good-quality early years services can have a positive impact on children's cognitive attainment at entry to school and may help to combat educational disadvantage. Given the available international evidence, it would be surprising if improvements were not seen in the UK.

The most thorough findings to date about the recent impact of early years services on children's development in the UK come from the Effective Provision of Pre-school Education (EPPE) programme.[9] This shows that pre-school education enhances children's development and that disadvantaged children in particular can benefit from good-quality pre-school settings.

The EPPE research also shows that disadvantaged children especially benefit from good-quality pre-school settings if they attend centres that cater for a mixture of children from different social backgrounds. The earlier children attend pre-school education, the more significant the gains to their intellectual development, independence, concentration and sociability. Where settings view educational and social development as complementary and equal in importance, children make better all round progress.

The EPPE findings are also reflected in other UK research. The evaluation of the early excellence centres pilot programme[10] reported case studies which indicated that the centres could help reduce social exclusion through enhanced social, emotional and cognitive development; early remediation of special needs and improved inclusion rates in mainstream settings; a reduction in rates of child protection orders and 'looked after' children; and improved physical well-being. But further research is necessary to provide more robust evidence about the impact of childcare services on the development of children living in poverty. Evidence that will be collected as part of the neighbourhood nurseries initiative evaluation project, for example, will include quality assessment of nursery provision and evidence about child outcomes.

## The challenges ahead

With one childcare place for every five children under the age of eight, early years services are still not reaching many families. One-quarter of all families report that they are not able to find a childcare place when they need it.[11]

Families at risk of poverty and social exclusion are still less likely to have access to early years' services. Use of early years' services remains closely related to parental work status and, related to this, ability to pay; parents who are unemployed or in training are least likely to have access to childcare. Although greater support is directed at low-income families through targeted initiatives, since the majority of early years services are part of a market system, they are more likely to be used by better-off families. Targeting provision by geographical area also has limited reach; only 54 per cent of poor children live in the 20 per cent most disadvantaged areas,[12] for example. For this reason Sure Start is still failing to reach nearly half of all poor children.

In addition, most studies report that ethnic minority families are less likely to have access (or use) early years services. The 2002 *Repeat Study of Parents' Demand for Childcare*[13] found that 87 per cent of White parents accessed some form of registered childcare in the previous year compared with 81 per cent of Black parents, 70 per cent of Asian parents and 71 per cent of other ethnic minority groups.

A Daycare Trust study,[14] which gathered views of 180 parents from ethnic minority communities, found that barriers to using childcare included: lack of trust in services; concerns about lack of culturally-appropriate services; lack of information; expense; services not fitting with working patterns; racism and prejudice; inflexibility of services (for example, childcare structures for different age groups seen as inappropriate by traveller families); and feeling isolated in the local community.

There is also evidence of insufficient childcare catering for children with special needs. One study found that 79 per cent of parents of a child with a disability have found it difficult to combine working and caring for their child because of childcare problems and 74 per cent of parents of a disabled child have had to cut back or give up work because of childcare problems.[15]

Families working atypical hours also face particular difficulties finding suitable childcare, despite the fact that most parents now work atypical hours: 53 per cent of mothers and 79 per cent of fathers now work some hours outside 9am to 5pm, Monday to Friday.[16] There is limited childcare provision for parents who work atypical hours and those providers that have sought to provide such a service have faced problems finding staff to work at these times.[17]

Despite recent improvements, therefore, the UK childcare system remains patchy and inflexible in terms of meeting the needs of different families who face a high risk of poverty and are least likely to have access to services.

The most significant factor in families' lack of access to childcare is market failure. For parents, cost is still perceived to be the biggest barrier. The typical cost of a full-time nursery place for a child under two is around £134 a week, almost £7,000 a year.[18] The cost of a childcare place has continued to rise well above inflation; the Daycare Trust's 2004 childcare costs survey revealed a 5 per cent rise in the previous year. Parents in the UK meet a higher proportion of childcare costs than in many countries; on average, parents in the Organisation for Economic Cooperation and Development (OECD) countries contribute 25-30 per cent of the overall costs of provision. Some countries, such as Sweden and Denmark, have set a maximum level for parental contributions, prohibiting services charging parents above this amount.

But cost is not the only factor. The lack of supply of childcare is also a major constraint. Despite growth in private nursery provision, one in four families are not able to find a childcare place when they need it. Childminding places have actually fallen in the past decade. The childcare market is experiencing problems of sustainability. Over the last year in London boroughs, for example, one nursery closed for every four that opened and one out-of-school club closed for every two that opened.[19] There is a particular difficulty sustaining services in deprived areas.[20] The Government's Strategy Unit report[21] noted that deprived wards have an average of six to eight places per 1,000 children aged 0-14, compared with an average of 12-14 places across all wards. There is also some evidence of places in disadvantaged areas being used by those from less disadvantaged areas.[22]

Absence of provision is compounded by parents' lack of knowledge about the services that do exist. Parents also report difficulties gaining access to information about local childcare services and only 3 per cent of parents use local children's information services.[23]

The availability of the childcare tax credit has yet to have a clear impact on the supply of provision. Although tax credits have helped those who are eligible to claim them, eligibility remains limited. Of those receiving the working tax credit, only 14 per cent of couple families and 23 per cent of lone-parent families are currently receiving the childcare tax credit.[24]

The cost and lack of supply of childcare mean that many families regularly rely on informal help from families and friends. Seventy per cent of employed women with dependent children use informal childcare for all or part of their childcare. This has led to calls for informal care to be better supported through the childcare tax credit by encouraging informal carers to register as child providers.[25] Given the importance of maintaining high quality provision in order to benefit children, especially the most disadvantaged, the Government has resisted calls for unregistered informal provision to be eligible for the childcare tax credit.

## The way forward

Attempts to address market failure, by contributing towards the childcare costs of low-income families and by investing in the supply of services in deprived areas, have so far been insufficient to ensure the growth of affordable and sustainable services on a scale necessary to meet the needs of all families.

The Government could step up its action to address market failure. Increasing the coverage of services to the most disadvantaged 30 per cent of areas, for example, would reach 70 per cent of the poorest children. Improvements could also be made to the childcare tax credit by raising the percentages of costs met, increasing support for larger families or extending support to those who are unemployed or working less than 16 hours a week.

But ultimately the UK has to consider whether it is possible to build a flexible, comprehensive, affordable, equitable system of early years provision with such a heavy reliance on market provision. Countries that have achieved near-universal access to childcare provision have done so through substantial and sustained public investment. The proportion of

GDP that Denmark spends on its early years services, for example, is nearly six times that of the UK.

A market system inherently works against the interests of the poor: the best-quality childcare is priced at levels beyond the reach of low-income families. A market system of childcare dependent almost entirely on parental contributions may also struggle to provide the kind of quality of service that is needed to enhance children's development; for-profit organisations can only make a profit by raising parental contributions or by adopting the lowest possible standards allowed under existing regulations.

The Government's vision for a children's centre in every community offers the prospect of universal, integrated services combining care and education, health and family support. For parents, having a children's centre within reach that caters for a wide range of needs, regardless of their financial or employment circumstances, would provide the kind of support that most families claim is woefully lacking in their community.

If such provision was affordable for low-income families, it could make a substantial contribution to reducing child poverty, both by helping to increase parental employment (and family income) and by enhancing children's development. The route to such a vision, however, does not lie in incremental steps to address market failure. It requires a substantial investment in the early years, an investment that is in keeping with a society committed to achieving greater social justice.

## Notes

1   The strategy applied only to policy in England and the devolved administrations took responsibility for childcare following the constitutional reforms of 1999. But the main elements of the strategy were subsequently adopted throughout the UK, albeit with differences later emerging as a result of action taken by the devolved administrations.

2   These are to increase the proportion of young children under five with normal levels of personal, social and emotional development; reduce the proportion of mothers who smoke during pregnancy; increase the proportion of children having normal levels of communication, language and literacy at the end of the Foundation Stage; increase the proportion of two-year-olds with satisfactory speech and language development at age two and reduce the number of children living in no-work households.

3   *Delivering for Children and Families: inter-departmental childcare review*, November 2002

4   Gordon Brown, Pre-Budget Report speech, 10 December 2003

5 *Towards Universal Childcare*, Daycare Trust, October 2003

6 *Changing the Landscape: lessons from the New Opportunities Fund out-of-school hours childcare programme*, New Opportunities Fund, 2003

7 Figures from the Labour Force Survey; see One Parent Families, *One Parent Families Today: the facts*, 2003

8 Department for Work and Pensions, *Opportunity for All*, The Stationery Office, 2003

9 K Sylva and others, *The Effective Provision of Pre-school Education (EPPE) Project: findings from the pre-school period*, 2003, www.ioe.ac.uk/cdl/eppe;

10 T Bertram and others, *Early Excellence Centre Pilot Programme Report 2000-01*, Department for Education and Skills Research Report RR361, 2002

11 S Woodland, M Millar and S Tipping, *Repeat Study of Parents' Demand for Childcare*, Department for Education and Skills Research Report 348, 2002

12 Work and Pensions Select Committee Report, 2003

13 See note 11

14 Daycare Trust, *Parents' Eye: building a vision of equality and inclusion in childcare services*, 2003

15 Contact a Family, *Contact a Family Childcare Survey*, 2002

16 I La Valle, S Arthur, C Millward, J Scott and M Clayden, *Happy Families? Atypical work and its influence on family life*, Joseph Rowntree Foundation Findings 982, 2002

17 J Statham and A Mooney, *Around the Clock: childcare services at atypical times*, Joseph Rowntree Foundation, 2003

18 Daycare Trust, *Childcare Costs Survey*, www.daycaretrust.org.uk, 2004

19 *The Sustainability of Childcare in London*, a joint report by the Greater London Enterprise and the Daycare Trust, January 2004.

20 Personal communication – early findings from the neighbourhood nurseries initiative implementation study, wave 1.

21 *Delivering for Families and Children*, Strategy Unit, Cabinet Office, 2002

22 T Smith, K Coxon, C Lee and H McColm, *Neighbourhood, Disadvantage and Childcare: Birmingham childcare research project*, unpublished report, 2002

23 See note 22

24 Inland Revenue, *Child and Working Tax Credits Quarterly Statistics*, January 2004

25 *Informal Childcare: bridging the childcare gap for families*, Daycare Trust / One Parent families, 2003

# Five

# Employment and child poverty

*Alan Marsh and Sandra Vegeris*

## The evolution of a work-based family welfare policy

Full employment in the mid-1960s was thought to have all but abolished child poverty. Fewer than one in ten families with dependent children had incomes below the poverty line of half the national average, compared with three in ten today. Even the relatively few lone parents then had employment rates higher than today.[1]

Yet by the late 1960s it was already clear that there was a problem with low-wage single-earner families, especially those with more than two children. Rising out-of-work benefits and falling tax thresholds left many such families with small difference between their incomes in or out of work. No one was comfortable with the idea that benefits given to relieve need during periods of unemployment were acting as a disincentive to work.[2] Just as every generation seems to have to re-discover child poverty for itself, so the 1970s contemplated the return of in-work family poverty.

Chancellor Barber's response was to propose child tax credits for his 1971 Budget. He was told, as many who followed him, that this was a good idea in theory but impractical. As a temporary measure, he introduced instead family income supplement (FIS), which remained for 17 years. Despite the manifest inadequacies of FIS, withdrawing under some circumstances £1.20 of any new pound earned, this marked the start of what has proved an extraordinary British commitment to wage supplementation.

From 1988 the deficiencies of FIS were addressed in part by family credit, which offered higher rates of in-work benefit and lower qualifying hours. Research showed that family credit drew more lone parents into work, fitting short-hours jobs around school hours. It helped couples through temporary troughs of low income without recourse to unemployment. Take-up among eligible families was higher than feared and most families entitled to more than trivial amounts got money sooner or later.

New technology has since allowed in-work benefits to move to the Inland Revenue and evolve into the integrated tax credits introduced in stages during the past three years. These are underpinned by a national minimum wage, which, though set low, prevents too much of the wage subsidy finding its way to employers.[3] Tax credits remain the Government's main policy instrument to combat child poverty by minimising non-employment among their parents. By 'making work pay', tax credits are designed to provide enough incentive to work while meeting the increasing challenge of keeping low-paid families' standards of living in touch with those of the working majority. Transitions to work are smoothed by allowances that shore up income until their first wage slip arrives. For lone parents, the new opportunity to keep the full value of any child support payments from non-resident parents was especially helpful.

Wage supplementation was the first of the three pillars of welfare-to-work policy set in place. These three are:

- **Making work pay:** in-work tax credits plus transitional benefits.
- **Active case management:** through New Deal programmes, including increased requirements upon unemployed two-parent families to actively seek work. In the case of lone parents, there are now mandatory requirements to receive work-focussed advice and encouragement, delivered through new Jobcentre Plus offices, as well as the voluntary provisions of the New Deal for Lone Parents.
- **New services:** Sure Start is a complex series of provisions to improve early childrearing practices, as a local provision. It is linked to a National Childcare Strategy to improve the supply side of the central problem of providing acceptable alternative care while parents, especially lone parents, are at work.

The remainder of this chapter reviews evidence of the effectiveness of work-based family welfare policies and reflects on the continued contribution that work may make to the eradication of child poverty by 2020. The key issues are:

- Is work increasing among families with dependent children?
- Does such movement into work substantially increase income and raise families' standards of living?
- Can families remaining out of work be kept out of poverty too?

## Movement into work

The growth of worklessness among British parents between 1975 and 1995 repeatedly outpaced the development of policy. Among parents in couples, worklessness was cyclical and in this period remains low. Among lone parents, the problem grew unchecked for twenty years and remains high.

## Lone parents

The largest part of worklessness in households with dependent children is among lone-parent families.[4] By 1991, their employment rates had fallen to fewer than three in ten working the kind of hours that nowadays attract wage supplements (16 or more hours per week). Since then, their employment rates have recovered to a little under half (46 per cent) in work of 16 or more hours a week, with a further 10 per cent working part time. More than half of this 46 per cent receive working tax credit; more than three-quarters of those entering work do so.

However, this apparent improvement in employment rates is tempered by the context of rising total numbers of lone parents.[5] While the proportion in work and receiving wage supplements grew from 1988, the total number of lone-parent families out of work and receiving income support also grew. It has fallen since 1997 but only back to the number seen in 1991. Eleven years on, we still have more than 800,000 women bringing up children alone on an out-of-work benefit never designed for families to live on for very long periods.

It would be churlish to try to make a case that the policy of increasing wage supplementation and active case management has contributed little or nothing to this rise in employment among lone parents. A lone parent entering work at, say, the average of 23 hours a week at the minimum wage now receives typically as much from the Government as s/he does from her/his new employer; it is hard to see how s/he would manage without it.

Nevertheless, other factors have contributed independently of policy to the rise in lone parents' employment rates. For example:

- The economy improved generally and unemployment fell – though it may be fair to say that policy had something to do with a better economy too.

- More jobs became available that offered the flexible short-hours working that lone parents welcome because they can fit such work in around school hours.
- The lone-parent population has aged. Their average age rose from 31 ten years ago to 35 today. For a group where eight out of ten fit into the 25 to 50 age band, this was a huge rise.
- Being older, lone parents now have fewer children under age five (36 per cent, down from 47 per cent ten years ago). In addition, the school entry age fell to four years at the end of the 1990s.
- Lone parents participated in rising education levels. The proportion among them without any qualifications fell from a half to a quarter in eight years.

These changes – increasing numbers, ages and employment – have their origins in the same cause: slow outflow. Average duration in lone parenthood rose. For example, among the Policy Studies Institutes's earlier study of 900 lone parents interviewed at intervals between 1991 and 2001, only half had a new partner.[6]

The signals for the future are, therefore, mixed. If the numbers of lone parents go on rising, it is likely that the proportion in work will also rise. Policy has made *working* lone parenthood a viable option for all but those with the steepest barriers to overcome. Those who receive some child support payments (and half the working lone parents do) can expect a standard of living similar to that of most single-earner couples. This prospect is quite new and welcome. But this means of course that direct entry to lone parenthood by single working women is now much easier than in the past. Equally, mothers in couples may discover that an uncertain income from a husband can be replaced by increased tax credits were they to become a single parent instead. Thus more 'mainstream' families, with higher rates of employment may be drawn into spells of lone parenthood. But this would not of itself withdraw children from poverty since the same number will remain the children of out-of-work lone parents.

## Couples

Except in economic recessions, there is relatively small concern about long-term unemployment among couples with children. Their difficulties have centred instead on the adequacy of wages in work, especially for single-earner couples. Family credit improved their position and tax credits have offered more. Though still means-tested, child tax credits now run so far up the income distribution that the minimum child tax credit rate approaches universal entitlement. But the portion of the extra cash given for two adults in low-paid couples (the working tax credit component) is the same as that given for lone-parent families, so they can feel relatively poorer.

In 2002 just 6 per cent of couples were out of work.[7] Two-thirds of these couples have at least one parent (sometimes both) who is long-term sick or disabled and about a third receive disability benefits. Most of the rest are out of work only a short time. Thus, probably less than 2 per cent of couples with children are presently longer-term unemployed in the traditional sense of seeking work and failing to find it.

By contrast, 54 per cent of couples with children are now dual earners, which is becoming the aspirational form for British families. Nearly all the rest (40 per cent) are single-earner couples, but one in ten of these have the mother as their sole working partner. Almost a fifth of working couples that claimed working families' tax credit in 2001 based their claim on the mother's job. But quite a large number of single-earner couples remained below the 60 per cent of the median threshold, partly because their take-up rates for tax credits are lower than the rate among lone parents. So work may well be the best form of welfare and a family's first protection from poverty, but dual earning is a guarantee. When you combine these trends with efforts to get more lone mothers into work, it is increases in *women's* work that policy expects to raise the bulwark between a family and higher risks of poverty.

There is among couples a strong link between child poverty and ethnicity. Pakistani and Bangladeshi couples have larger families and usually rely on low single-earner wages. Their incomes are so compressed that Bangladeshi families who are better off than 90 per cent of other Bangladeshi families still have incomes below the White average. They are far more prone to hardship too.

## The impact of work upon family living standards

### Measuring hardship

Researching changes in the living standards of families with children from year to year provides a means for monitoring child poverty.[9] The Families and Children Study includes items from which a hardship index has been constructed.

Hardship here means 'going without' things that most people acknowledge families should not go without, and incorporates being unable to repay debt and living in unacceptably poor housing. The index considers three dimensions of living across nine measures.[10]

1. **Accommodation**. The family:
   - has three or more problems with housing *and* is unable to afford repairs, if a homeowner;
   - lives in overcrowded accommodation;
   - cannot afford adequate heating.
2. **Finances**. The family:
   - has no bank account *and* two or more problem debts that cannot be serviced;
   - worries about money almost all the time and runs out of money most weeks.
3. **Expenditure**. The family goes without:
   - food items;
   - clothing items;
   - consumer durables;
   - social participation (including trips out, having friends home and holidays) because they cannot afford them.

A family satisfying any one of these is assigned a point on the hardship index, ranging from zero to a maximum of nine. Index scores are then categorised into a summary index:

| Score | Category |
|-------|----------|
| 0 | 'not in hardship' |
| 1–2 | 'moderate hardship' |
| 3–9 | 'severe hardship' |

## The incidence of hardship

This is a cautious, conservative measure of hardship. Thus, in 2002, 71 per cent of British families were not in hardship, 22 per cent were in moderate hardship and just 7 per cent were in severe hardship. However, families in severe hardship were concentrated among:

- out-of-work couple families (21 per cent in 'severe hardship');
- lone-parent families (16 per cent);
- families with three or more children (12 per cent); *and*
- ethnic minority families (13 per cent).

Since almost no one in a well-paid job registers a single point on the hardship index, our discussion below of the role of work in combating hardship focuses on moderate and low-income families.[11] Table 5.1 shows the proportion of working and non-working families in severe hardship for a large representative snapshot of families over four points in time, between 1999 and 2002.

In each year, severe hardship is concentrated among the worst-off families who were out of work or receiving tax credits, as you would expect. It is worth noting here how rates of severe hardship are very similar for lone-parent and couple families when their very different employment rates are accounted for.

However, work clearly helps since families on tax credits in 1999 were half as likely to be in severe hardship compared with the out-of-work families, and those with only moderate incomes had only small risks of severe hardship.

In the three years following the 1999 survey, something quite remarkable occurred. Severe hardship almost vanished among working families – lone parents and couples alike. This was partly due to the way

**Table 5.1: The proportion of low- and moderate-income families in 'severe hardship', by family type, and work and tax credit status**

|  | 1999 | 2000 | 2001 | 2002 |
|---|---|---|---|---|
|  | % | % | % | % |
| **Lone-parent families** | | | | |
| Not working | 41 | 37 | 28 | 26 |
| Tax credits | 21 | 12 | 10 | 6 |
| Moderate income | 4 | 2 | 3 | 2 |
| **Couple families** | | | | |
| Not working | 41 | 34 | 22 | 21 |
| Tax credits | 23 | 15 | 9 | 6 |
| Moderate income | 4 | 2 | 1 | 1 |

Source: Families and Children Study (1999-2002), cross-sectional data.

Note: Moderate income is defined as those families with incomes just above eligibility for tax credits.

tax credits (compared to family credit in 1999) gave extra money to the lowest paid and at the same time 'captured' more families who had higher incomes anyway. However, the extra money given at the same time through higher rates of income support, especially for the younger children, appears to have reduced rates of severe hardship among the out-of-work families too. Among couples, it halved, so by 2002 they stood on the same point on the scale as the family credit couples had stood only three years earlier.

This welcome development is tempered only by the way the falls in severe hardship among out-of-work families levelled off between 2001 and 2002, leaving more than one in five out-of-work families still experiencing severe hardship in 2002. Given that over half of lone parent families were out of (full-time) work in 2002, and their falls in hardship were smaller than for the couples, this remains a substantial challenge for child welfare policy. Hardship will remain at around this level unless out-of-work families receive substantially more cash or more of them move into work.

## The impact of entering work

Hardship falls when families enter work. Chart 5.1 tracks families who were not in work in 1999 but who were working 16 or more hours a week by 2001. Positive shifts were seen at both ends of the hardship index – the proportion of families experiencing severe hardship fell from about 30 to 10 per cent. Correspondingly, families who avoided hardship altogether almost doubled, from 27 to 50 per cent.

In greater detail, Chart 5.2 shows changes in the different measures comprising the hardship index for families who entered work between 1999 and 2001. Prior to work (1999), all but one of the factors (unaffordable heating) was an issue for more than 15 per cent of out-of-work families. After becoming a working household, hardship fell substantially on all but two of the factors. Here the magnitude of change is not as important as the areas of change. Newly working families reported they were much more capable of meeting the costs for food, clothing, consumer durables and social participation. Fewer of these families had worries about finances or problems with debts and more could afford the costs of heating. However, issues around the costs of accommodation – overcrowding and housing repairs – did not change. As a result, hardship for newly working families transformed from a more general construct to one focused on problems

**Chart 5.1: The distribution of hardship scores among families when they were out of work in 1999 and when they were in work of 16 or more hours a week in 2001**

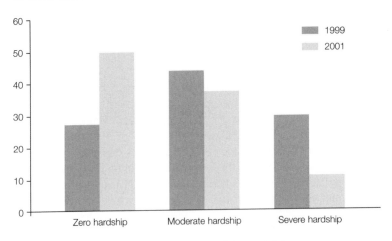

Source: Families and Children Study (1999–2001), panel data.
Sample: Low-to-moderate income families who were out of work (or working fewer than 16 hours a week) in 1999 but who had entered work of 16 hours a week or more when they were interviewed again in 2001.

with housing. Recent trends in the housing market do not encourage a view of better housing for poorer families. Problems with overcrowding will continue unless family sizes among the most disadvantaged fall.

## How much more work?

The Government's work-based family welfare policy now delivers £6.5 billion of *extra* money to British families each year, compared with the annual rate of subsidy in 1997. More families now work; nearly all couples and approaching half the lone parents have 'full-time' jobs and about a fifth of working families now receive wage supplements, whose cash value can match wages among the lowest paid. Even the out-of-work families are £40 a week better off in real terms. Sutherland, Sefton and Piachaud estimate that these changes will lift a quarter of families who would otherwise

**Chart 5.2: Changes in individual measures of hardship, before and after families entered work**

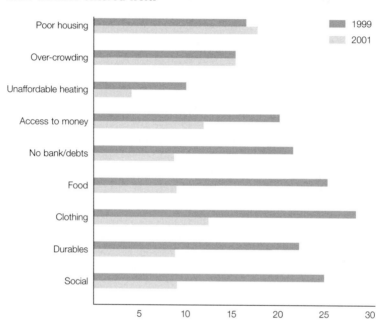

Source: Families and Children Study (1999–2001), panel data.
Sample: Low-to-moderate income families who were out of work (or working fewer than 16 hours a week) in 1999 but who had entered work of 16 hours a week or more when they were interviewed again in 2001.

have remained 'in poverty' above the threshold of 60 per cent of median income by 2004, meeting the Government's interim target.[12] We showed evidence above that real improvements in standards of living have accompanied these increases in income and employment.

However welcome these developments are, sympathetic sceptics such as Jonathan Bradshaw warn that '...the task is going to get harder'.[13] Easing a minority of poor children over an arbitrary threshold and reducing hardship has not yet been too costly in fiscal or political terms. Broad public sympathy for Labour's project has yet to be tested by the kind of taxation required to lift those deeper in poverty over the line and keep all children above it. The Institute for Fiscal Studies estimates that without extra tax-funded resources only a 'dramatic' increase in parents' earnings would meet the later targets of raising a half and then all poor children above the threshold.[14]

What scope remains, then, for a dramatic increase in earnings among British parents? It bears repeating that nearly all the extra work that will increase the income available to children and remove them from poverty is extra *women's* work. And much of this will be from lone parents, whose employment rates rose only slowly, from 29 per cent in 1991 to 46 per cent in 2002. Given the growth in flexible-hours employment, increased wage supplements (including larger childcare payments), and their increasing average age, it would have been amazing – not to say alarming – if their employment rates had not risen. It is possible to be surprised they did not rise more.

In this light, the Government's target to put '70 per cent of lone parents in work by 2010' also begins to look challenging. If it is to embrace part-time hours it may be easier to achieve but it will make a correspondingly weaker contribution to reducing child poverty. It also means that nearly all those lone parents who must get jobs to help the Government to its target are the ones with younger children. But we are no more likely to see 70 per cent of lone parents with pre-school children in full-time work than we will see 90-100 per cent of the lone mothers of teenagers in work. Already, those lone parents with only teenage children have employment rates close to those of older men (about 65 per cent). It seems hard to ask more of them, especially since those older lone parents that do not work usually have good reason. Many are unwell.

This initiative could be made stronger if more cash support were given for work below the working tax credit threshold of 16 hours a week than the present £20 earnings disregard. There is intuitively a case for easing lone mothers into work at lower hours anyway – this is what mothers in two-parent households do. Otherwise, in order to improve their families' living standards, lone parents need to jump straight into the working tax credit range beyond 16 hours a week. For enough to do so to meet the 70 per cent target they will need childcare provision of Scandinavian quality and scale and about 380,000 full-time jobs between them.

It is already the case that women who become lone parents as *workers* (single or married) usually stay in work. In the longer run, a policy that holds most promise for the improvement of children's living standards will begin by further strengthening women's position in the labour market, completing their integration into the labour market on equal terms with men. It may one day cease to be 'obvious' which parent supplies most of the earnings and which most of the care when children are young, even when parents do not live together. In new parental leave allowances, for example, we have the beginnings of policy that encourages balanced parenting and this may promise a lot in terms of children's long-term protection from poverty.

Meanwhile, it is worth remembering that the cohort of children just grown was caught in the maw of a dramatic growth in income inequality, which has left us with the present problem. Under Labour, wage inequality has not abated and may grow worse. And it will always remain the case that parents of young children, often young themselves, will tend to have lower earning capacity and greater needs, compared with households without children. It therefore seems sensible to concentrate for the while on keeping all children from hardship rather than becoming too attached to a longer goal of population-wide income equalities. There is evidence above that a good start has been made.

## Notes

1 By 1972 Britain had approximately 500,000 lone parents, a quarter of them widows, the remainder mostly divorced women with jobs.

2 An administrative device called the 'wage stop' prevented families receiving more in benefit than they had had in wages but did not count in-work expenses such as travel. This tended only to discriminate against the unusually low-paid, including disabled parents.

3 It is possible to argue, of course, that the extension of wage supplementation to all low-paid workers has turned the national minimum wage into a device that transfers a large part of its total cost to employers. Other advantages, though, including causing employers to value and train their workers more, and the pitiable wages still being recorded by some family credit claimants as late as 1999, have won all-party support for the national minimum wage.

4 There are more than 800,000 lone parents either not working or working less than 16 hours a week. This compares with about 300,000 out-of-work couples.

5 Lone parents grew in numbers from 500,000 to 1.7m today, or from 7 to 24 per cent of all families.

6 A Marsh and S Vegeris, *The British Lone Parent Cohort and their Children*, Department for Work and Pensions Research Report, 2004 (in press)

7 D Kasparova, A Marsh, S Vegeris and J Perry, *Families and Children 2001: work and childcare*, Department for Work and Pensions Report 191, Corporate Document Services, 2003, Table 2.1, p32

8 See R Berthoud, 'Poverty and Prosperity Among Britain's Ethnic Minorities', *Benefits* 33:10 (1), 2002; A Marsh and J Perry, *Black and Ethnic Minority Children and Poverty*, National Children's Bureau, 2003

9  This approach has now been incorporated into the Government's planned programme of research to measure progress towards the elimination of child poverty. See *Measuring Child Poverty*, Department for Work and Pensions, 2003

10 For more details on the construction of the hardship index, which derives from
   80 separate measures, refer to Appendix E in S Vegeris and J Perry, *Families
   and Children 2001: living standards and the children*, Department for Work and
   Pensions Research Report 190, Corporate Documents Services, 2003

11 'Moderate and low-income families' are out of work, working and eligible for
   working tax credits, or have a total family income 10 per cent above the point
   at which their eligibility for working tax credit runs out

12 H Sutherland, T Sefton and D Piachaud, *Poverty in Britain: the impact of
   government policy since 1997*, Joseph Rowntree Foundation, 2003

13 J Bradshaw, 'Child Poverty Under Labour', in G Fimister (ed) *Tackling Child
   Poverty in the UK: An end in sight?*, Child Poverty Action Group, 2001

14 M Brewer, T Clark and A Goodman, *The Government's Child Poverty Target:
   How much progress has been made?*, Institute for Fiscal Studies, 2002

# Six

# Ending child poverty: a matter of human rights, citizenship and social justice

*Ruth Lister*

> We must give all our children the opportunity to achieve their hopes and fulfil their potential. By investing in them, we are investing in our future.[1]

> Poverty denies children their fundamental human rights.[2]

These two quotations provide contrasting, yet potentially complementary, justifications for according the commitment to eradicate child poverty the highest priority. The first draws explicitly on the idea of children as an investment and implicitly on notions of social justice. The second appeals to a discourse of human rights, which translates also into a language of children's rights and citizenship. This chapter will discuss these different philosophical rationales. It will argue that each of them plays a valuable part in the overall case for tackling child poverty, but that the Government's emphasis on children as *investments* needs to be balanced by a more explicit appeal to principles of social justice and to the human rights of children *qua children*.

## Social justice

In his 'Beveridge revisited' lecture, in which he made the commitment to eradicate child poverty, Tony Blair declared that social justice remains 'our central belief – the basis for a community where everyone has the chance to succeed'.[3] Views differ as to whether our understanding of social justice today should be rooted in more egalitarian, or more meritocratic, principles, in other words whether the prime objective is greater equality or greater equality of opportunity. Whichever the model preferred, child poverty represents a violation of social justice. Children in poverty are the victims of an unjust distribution of society's resources both as between income groups and as between those with and those without children. As a result, their opportunity to fulfil their potential is severely restricted. In the words of a recent Institute for Public Policy Research report, 'all those who wish to achieve a more socially just society must concern themselves with reducing the unequal life chances that emerge soon after birth'.[4]

For those who subscribe to a more egalitarian model of social justice, it is not enough to argue for the redistribution of opportunities to children in poverty through, for example, education. As Anthony Giddens, a proponent of the redistribution of opportunities over resources, has acknowledged, in an unequal society 'the privileged are bound to be able to confer advantages on their children – thus destroying meritocracy'.[5] Moreover, at the bottom of the ladder, the evidence suggests that poverty makes it difficult, if well nigh impossible, for some children to grasp the opportunities being offered to them. A study by the Centre for Economic Performance found that social and economic disadvantage was the most important factor hindering the development of basic literacy and numeracy skills. It concluded that arguably the most powerful educational policy would tackle child poverty directly. At its most basic, hungry children do not make good learners.[6]

## Investing in children

Although the Government's commitment to tackle child poverty is inspired by a continued belief in social justice, this tends to be more implicit than explicit in its public pronouncements on the issue. Instead, as exemplified by the quotation from Gordon Brown that heads this chapter, these tend to be couched in a language of investment: investment in children and in our own futures. This language is more compatible with 'third way' thinking than the traditional social democratic language of 'tax and spend'. It is a politically powerful language in its attempt to appeal to the enlightened self-interest of all members of society and in its implicit acknowledgement of the need to provide the resources to give children in poverty the same 'chance to succeed' as other children. Indeed, it is a language that CPAG has itself deployed on many an occasion in its attempts to gain public and political support for tackling child poverty in a society that is not that child-friendly.[7]

However, there are dangers in placing too much emphasis on children as investments as the justification for tackling child poverty. The orientation is towards the future rather than the present. In contrast, what has been called a 'new paradigm' of childhood sees children primarily as 'beings' rather than 'becomings'.[8] Seeing children as 'beings' means paying attention to their current well-being and to the quality of their childhood as well as to their future life chances, crucial as they are. This is reflected in a United Nations (UN) statement to which the UK is a signatory. It offers a vision of:

> ...a world in which all girls and boys can enjoy childhood – a time of play and learning, in which they are loved, respected and cherished, their rights are promoted and protected, without discrimination of any kind, where their safety and well-being are paramount, and where they can develop in health, peace and dignity.

The kind of evidence presented in Chapter One of this volume, which provides children's own perspectives on the impact of poverty, is a powerful reminder of why we should be concerned about what poverty does to childhood which, after all, is only lived once. The same conclusion was reached by the recent Save the Children report into severe and persistent poverty.[10]

The 'children as investments' approach also runs the risk of instrumentality: children become instruments for achieving the Government's economic and social goals rather than ends in their own right as human beings. This is exemplified in the Treasury's observation that, because poverty affects both childhood and children's 'experience as adults and the life chances of their own children', 'support for today's disadvantaged children will therefore help to ensure a more flexible economy tomorrow'.[11] As I have argued elsewhere, this approach constructs the child as the 'citizen-worker of the future', a cipher for future economic prosperity.[12] In doing so it risks losing sight of the child *qua* child and of the child-citizen as the bearer of human rights.

## Human rights

According to a report published by the UN Office of the High Commissioner for Human Rights, 'poverty is the principal cause of human rights violations in the world'.[13] A human rights conceptualisation of poverty, the Office of the High Commissioner contends:

> leads to more adequate responses to the many facets of poverty… It gives due attention to the critical vulnerability and subjective daily assaults on human dignity that accompany poverty. Importantly, it looks not just at resources but also at the capabilities, choices, security and power needed for enjoyment of an adequate standard of living and other fundamental civil, cultural, political and social rights.[14]

This statement contains two principles that are central to the case for tackling poverty, including child poverty. First is that of human dignity. 'Respect for the inherent dignity of all members of the human family'[15] lies at the heart of human rights thinking. Entitlement to 'the economic, social and cultural rights indispensable to [human] dignity' is enshrined in Article 22 of the Universal Declaration of Human Rights. The UN General Assembly has warned that 'extreme poverty and social exclusion constitute a violation of human dignity'.[16]

The indignities suffered by parents and children living in poverty are frequently mentioned as one of the aspects of poverty that is hardest to bear. In one study published by CPAG, a mother explained that 'poverty strips your dignity. You can't have any dignity with poverty'.[17] The Commission on Poverty, Participation and Power commented that 'the lack of respect for people living in poverty was one of the clearest and most heartfelt messages which came across to us as a Commission'.[18] Research directly with children underlines how they feel the shame of poverty particularly keenly as they struggle, in Tess Ridge's words, to 'fit in' and 'join in' and not be seen as 'different'.[19] In a Children's Rights Alliance study, which talked to children living in deprived areas, the discussions were all 'woven with the threads of stigma and shame'.[20] Unfortunately, shock advertising, however well intended, is likely to encourage the stigmatisation of families in poverty as 'other' rather than the dignifying and respectful treatment a human rights perspective calls for. An example is the recent controversial advertising campaign by Barnardo's, which used images such as a new-born baby with a cockroach or syringe in its mouth and which talked of babies in poverty facing a 'future of squalor'.[21]

The second principle underpinning the human rights conceptualisation of poverty quoted above is that of the 'indivisibility' or 'interdependence' of human rights: 'the fact that the enjoyment of some rights may be dependent on or contribute to the enjoyment of others'.[22] Thus, strengthening social rights in the form of access to an adequate income may bolster the ability of parents and children (in some instances when older) to exercise civil and political rights. It also enhances the capacity to exercise parental responsibilities.

## Citizenship

The balance between rights and responsibilities lies at the heart of many contemporary political debates about citizenship. Although children are not full citizens as defined in terms of the formal rights and obligations of citizenship, some exercise informal citizenship responsibilities such as informal voluntary work in the local community or as young carers. Moreover, their material well-being depends, in part, on adequate social rights of citizenship that come to them indirectly through the adults responsible for their care. Thus, tackling child poverty also means tackling family poverty. In particular it means addressing the poverty experienced by mothers who often act as the shock absorbers of poverty, as they attempt to protect their children from poverty's full impact.

Citizenship is at heart about membership. Although children's relationship to citizenship is different from that of adults, they are still members of the citizen community. Membership involves not just the relationship between individuals and the state, but also the relationships between individual members of a citizenship community. It is about the ability to participate fully in society. A study published by CPAG a decade ago highlighted

> the emphasis which both parents and children place on 'participation': the right of every child to share in the activities, experiences and lifestyle of the community in which s/he is born and brought up. In a materialistic world, the ability of a child to participate is predicated to a large extent on access to goods, services and activities, all of which have a financial cost.

It continued:

> the determination that children should be able to 'participate' and its negative corollary, the fear of exclusion, are of equal importance to parents and children alike. Yet it is equally apparent that many parents must be unable to meet the financial demands which 'participation' involves, however skilfully they juggle resources or however great their own sacrifices.[23]

A very similar picture was painted by Ridge's more recent study, which underlined the financial costs of participation and the social and psychological costs to both children and parents in poverty of children's inability to participate.[24] Poverty inhibits full and equal participation in society, leading to second-class citizenship and social exclusion.

## Children's rights

Ridge's study emphasised the importance of seeing children as active agents in their own lives rather than as the passive objects of adult scrutiny and concern. This conceptualisation of children informs 'the demand that children be included in citizenship [which] is simply a request that children be seen as members of society too, with a legitimate and valuable voice and perspective'.[25]

The UN Convention on the Rights of the Child legitimates such a reading of children's status. A number of the rights enshrined in the Convention are jeopardised by poverty even in an affluent industrialised society like the UK, as illustrated in previous chapters. They include the right to:

- 'the enjoyment of the highest attainable standard of health' (Article 24);
- 'a standard of living adequate for the child's physical, mental, spiritual, moral and social development' (Article 27);
- 'engage in play and recreational activities appropriate to the age of the child and to participate freely in cultural life and the arts' (Article 31).

The Children's Rights Development Unit has observed that 'fulfilment of the right of every child to a standard of living for 'mental, spiritual, moral and social development' requires that children are provided, through their families, with sufficient resources to feel themselves to be part of society'.[26] Instead, poverty all too often spells exclusion and marginalisation.

Article 12 of the Convention enshrines the child's right to express an opinion and to have that opinion taken into account in any matter or procedure affecting the child. More generally, draft UN guidelines assert that 'a human rights approach to poverty reduction...requires active and informed participation by the poor in the formulation, implementation and monitoring of poverty reduction strategies'.[27] Calls for the voices of people in poverty to be heard in policy making and campaigning are becoming more vocal in the UK.

The message is slowly beginning to be taken on board by the Government. In its consultations on measuring child poverty, for instance, the Department for Work and Pensions held workshops with both children and parents with experience of poverty. In a report on its preliminary conclusions, it acknowledges that the children's 'views were extremely informative in bringing a different perspective to our understanding'.[29] The *United Kingdom National Action Plan on Social Inclusion 2003-05* states that 'the recognition that people with a direct experience of poverty have much to offer a successful anti-poverty strategy is beginning to transform the UK's approach. This participative approach...provides further impetus to the fight against exclusion'.[30]

The participatory approach was in line with one of the objectives established by the European Commission for member states' Action Plans. A participation working group has been established to advise the Government. Its stated aim is:

> To enable people in poverty to participate in the development of the UK NAP 2005 and beyond by establishing a real partnership between people living in poverty (women, men and children from different backgrounds) and government at all levels in order to improve the anti-poverty policy and practice described in the NAP.[31]

While participation so far has been limited, the principle has at least been acknowledged and if the working group's broader goal were achieved, it could indeed be transformative in its impact.

In sum, the argument here is that a citizenship and human rights approach not only provides an important justification for the eradication of child poverty but also recognises children as active rights-bearers whose voices need to be heard.

## Conclusion

The case for ending child poverty in a generation, as promised by Tony Blair five years ago, rests on a number of important principles, not all of which are necessarily articulated by the Government itself. The Government tends to place most emphasis on tackling child poverty as an investment – in children themselves and in all our futures. It is a powerful argument that has a political resonance, particularly if coupled with an explicit appeal to principles of social justice. However, on its own it runs the risk of treating children as the means to a better society and economy in the future rather than as ends in their own right in the present. The invocation of the philosophy of citizenship, human rights and children's rights serves to remind us that child poverty is 'a scar on Britain's soul'[32] not only because of its future effects but also because it denies children their full rights *as children* and as child-citizen members of our society.

## Notes

1  G Brown, 'A Scar on the Nation's Soul', *Poverty* 104, 1999, p8

2  D Gordon, S Nandy, C Pantazis, S Pemberton and P Townsend, *Child Poverty in the Developing World*, Policy Press, 2003, p1

3  T Blair, 'Beveridge Revisited: a welfare state for the 21st century', reproduced in R Walker (ed), *Ending Child Poverty*, Policy Press, 1999, p8

4  L Harker and L Kendall, *An Equal Start*, Institute for Public Policy Research, 2003, p62

5  A Giddens, *The Third Way*, Polity Press, 1998, p102

6  P Robinson, *Literacy, Numeracy and Economic Performance*, Centre for Economic Performance

7  See R Lister, 'The Politics of Child Poverty in Britain from 1965 to 1990', *Revue Française de Civilisation Britannique*, XI (1), pp67-80

8  See B Fawcett, B Featherstone and J Goddard, *Contemporary Child Care Policy and Practice*, Palgrave, forthcoming; A Prout, 'Children's Participation: control and self-realisation in British late modernity', *Children and Society* 14, pp304-15

9  United Nations, *A World Fit for Children*, 2002. Resolution adopted by the General Assembly 27th Special Session, para 9 (emphasis added)

10 L Adelman, S Middleton and K Ashworth, *Britain's Poorest Children: severe and persistent poverty and social exclusion*, Save the Children, 2003

11 HM Treasury, *Budget Report 2003*, HM Treasury, para 5.4

12 R Lister, 'Investing in the Citizen-workers of the Future', *Social Policy and Administration*, 37(5), pp427-43

13 *Human Rights and Extreme Poverty*, report submitted by A M Lazin, independent expert to the Commission on Human Rights, 55th session of the Economic and Social Council, E/CN.4/1999/48, 29 January 1999

14 Office of the High Commissioner for Human Rights, *What is Poverty?*, 2002, www.unhchr.ch/development/poverty-02.html

15 Office of the High Commissioner for Human Rights, *Draft Guidelines: a human rights approach to poverty reduction strategies*, OHCHR, 2002, p42

16 UN General Assembly, *Vienna Declaration and Programme of Action*, United Nations, 1993, para 25

17 P Beresford, D Green, R Lister and K Woodard, *Poverty First Hand*, Child Poverty Action Group, 1999, p90

18 Commission on Poverty, Participation and Power, *Listen Hear: the right to be heard*, Policy Press, 2000, p3

19 T Ridge, *Childhood Poverty and Social Exclusion*, Policy Press, 2002 and see Chapter 1 of this volume

20 C Willow, *Bread is Free: children and young people talk about poverty*, Children's Rights Alliance for England, 2001, p12

21 The full-page advertisements, the first of which appeared on 12 November 2003, drew widespread criticism (*The Guardian*, 13 November). For a discussion of how media images can serve to 'other' those in poverty see R Lister, *Poverty*, Polity Press, 2004 forthcoming.

22 See note 15, p2

23 S Middleton, K Ashworth and R Walker, *Family Fortunes*, Child Poverty Action Group, 1994, pp146 and 150

24 See note 19

25 J Roche, 'Children: rights, participation and citizenship', *Childhood*, 6(4), pp 475-93

26 G Lansdown (ed), *UK Agenda for Children*, Children's Rights Development Unit, 1994, p87. The CDRU was an independent project set up in the 1990s to encourage the fullest possible implementation of the Convention on the Rights of the Child in the UK.

27 See note 15

28 See note 18

29 Department for Work and Pensions, *Measuring Child Poverty Consultation: preliminary conclusions*, DWP, 2003, p15

30 Department for Work and Pensions, *United Kingdom National Action Plan on Social Inclusion 2003-05*, DWP, 2003, p1

31 See note 29, Annex F, p90

32 See note 1

# Seven

# Ending child poverty by 2020: the first five years

*Paul Dornan*

This final chapter takes the title of the book itself: *Ending Child Poverty by 2020: the first five years*. We have had five years, but the goal is still some way off. This chapter provides an overview of the progress so far – drawing on each of the contributions – and discusses future prospects. The overall argument of this book is relatively simple: much has been done, but more policy effort and redistribution is needed if the Government is to reach the excellent ambition of ending child poverty.

## Why are we reducing child poverty?

The first and previous chapters, those of Tess Ridge and Ruth Lister give a particular – distinct – angle on this question. Why are we concerned about childhood poverty? There are two central concerns for why we might reduce child poverty, both fundamental: echoing Lister, those of 'equality' and of 'equality of opportunity'. The first suggests policies of the sort that Ridge in particular advocates, which are child focused and start from the premise that the concerns of children, reported by children, should be the central concern for policy. The second suggests policies directed at improving outcomes, ensuring the best possible start for a child – on the road to becoming an adult.

Both of these are good reasons for reducing child poverty: government ought to intervene to improve both the lives and the chances of children. It is likely that policies aiming to achieve the former will improve the latter (for instance through improved nutrition, development and educational attainment). The importance of the distinction is most apparent in the way in which it is the underlying motivation conditioning the sorts of policies chosen. In terms of a practical example, Tess Ridge offers us the child trust fund, a vehicle through which the Treasury will invest on behalf of children and which aims to provide an asset at age 18. The child trust fund is intended to facilitate choice in young adulthood and plays heavily, therefore, to the equality of opportunity argument: it is about life chances of children (or rather, of young adults). Money invested, however, cannot be touched until the young person's 18th birthday. The child trust fund will have no impact on the family income while its owner is a child, however destitute the family, and therefore the child, may be: the policy has no impact on the lives of children as children.

The most important motivation behind policy ought, therefore, to be to ensure that families have adequate resources whilst children are growing up. The same principle lies behind the distinction between where new resources should be spent: on improving family income or on providing better services. Again, this should not be seen an either/or situation; both are essential. If the emphasis is, however, placed on service investment at the expense of that of improving family income, this will tacitly imply that current family incomes are sufficient to ensure current adequate dignity. Whilst we have the evidence of the detrimental impact of inadequate financial resources that Tess Ridge recounts, together with that of Alan Marsh and Sandra Vegeris on severe hardship (falling but still unacceptably high), it is plain enough that this has not been achieved.

## Making progress and making a difference

On 18 March 1999 Tony Blair made the promise to end child poverty in 20 years. Subsequent clarification established the bones of a strategy, on route to ending child poverty (by 2020). It was to be halved by 2010 and to have fallen by a quarter by 2004/05, the first milestone year. The precise measurement of this – as set out in the Department for Work and Pensions' Public Service Agreement (PSA)[1] – implies a specific definition of child income poverty (up to 2004/05). Children have been defined as poor if they live in households with an equivalised[2] needs-adjusted income below 60 per cent of the national median between the measurement year of 1998/99 and the milestone year of 2004/05.[3] Table 7.1 sets out the data for the base year (1998/99), the latest available *Households Below Average Income* data and the official target implied by the PSA.

Significant attention has been paid to whether the Government is on course to meet its target for reducing child poverty. Whether it will or not is difficult to judge. It looks likely to meet the target on the 'before housing costs' measure, but it is too close to call whether the target will have

**Table 7.1: Income poverty rates and target in Great Britain, millions (% of children)**

|  | Before housing costs | After housing costs |
|---|---|---|
| 1998/99 | 3.1 (24) | 4.2 (33) |
| 2001/02 | 2.7 (21) | 3.8 (30) |
| *2004/05 official target* | *2.3 (18)* | *3.2 (25)* |

Source: Office for National Statistics, *Households Below Average Income 1994/95-2001/02*, Department for Work and Pensions, 2003, p65

been met on the 'after housing costs' measure (the Government has further to go). Projecting the effects of income redistribution is an inexact science. Analysts not only have to explore the impacts of policy change, but also the effects of interactions with other income sources and with overall national median income. Analysts do not always reach the same conclusions and usually attach a degree of caution to their findings. Nevertheless, findings are informative, and we have related research from the Institute for Fiscal Studies (IFS) and the work of Holly Sutherland and others, funded by the Joseph Rowntree Foundation (JRF) that examines progress in tackling child income poverty.

The JRF research, the final report[4] of which was published in autumn 2003, was very encouraging, concluding that, on the basis of what was known and all other things being equal, the Government would meet its target on the before and after housing costs measures. The IFS published a series of related pieces of research[5] which were more down-beat, indicating that more needed to be done to ensure that the Government would meet its target on both the before and after housing cost measures. The last piece of research predicted the need for an additional 1 billion pounds of expenditure going into the child tax credit in order for the Government to meet its first milestone. The December 2003 pre-Budget Report promised an additional £885 million to be spent on the per child element of the child tax credit, worth about £2.50 per child per week on top of earnings inflation.[6] Though less than asked for, and made less generous by the combined effect of a concurrent freeze in the family and disability elements of the child tax credit, it was enough for the IFS to say that the Government *might just hit its poverty target*.[7]

Whether or not the first target is met, both the IFS and JRF analyses emphasise that the second target – that of halving child poverty by 2010 – is a more difficult proposition. More than this, we should be careful about targets. Even if both the first and second milestones are reached, Sutherland and others note in their final paragraph that 'relative poverty will still be higher than in 1979… Britain at the beginning of the twenty-first century remains a nation scarred by poverty.'[8] The roots of economic disadvantage that produce the high rates of child poverty we see in the UK are entrenched. It is understandable that Tony Blair suggested a 20-year time frame and there has been a consensus that this is a reasonable period in which to deal with so intractable a problem. The implication of this time scale is that for years to come many children will continue to grow up in poverty, with all of its adverse associations. The target should not only be to meet the proposed targets, it should be to break them. The Chancellor indicated a desire to 'advance faster'[9] against the child poverty targets in his Budget 2003. Ensuring that this occurs should be a job central to the 2004 Spending Review and beyond.

We do not just have income analysis to rely on, but the more tangible analysis of hardship provided by Alan Marsh and Sandra Vegeris. This analysis is more focused on outcomes of policy – the living conditions of families – than the income measures discussed above. The two are, though, clearly related and tell a similar picture. Just as income poverty has been falling so too has hardship and severe hardship. Chapter Five gives a fuller analysis of the patterns. The Marsh and Vegeris analysis takes us from 1999 to 2002. Using a composite measure the authors describe as a 'cautious, conservative measure of hardship', they show severe hardship was very high in 1999. About two-fifths of not-working lone-parent families and not-working couple families suffered severe hardship in 1999. By 2002 this had fallen to about a quarter of lone parents and a fifth of couple families. Still unacceptably high, but much lower than in 1999. For those in receipt of tax credits in 1999 just over a fifth were in severe hardship in 1999, but by 2002 this had fallen to about one in 20. Marsh and Vegeris ascribe the causation of this to the combined effect of increased employment and tax credits. They demonstrate clear progress, but caution is required on a number of grounds. Firstly, this was a conservative measure (families missing out on more than three out of a list of nine necessities) – we ought to be aiming higher. Secondly, progress was most pronounced between 1999 and 2001; after 2001 progress slowed. Further, for workless families the level of severe hardship (a quarter for lone parents and a fifth for couple families) 'will remain at around this level unless out-of-work families receive substantially more cash or more of them move into work'.

So the combined strategy of increased employment and redistribution has, on the whole, proved successful. It has delivered increases in the incomes of the poorest, reduced the numbers of children in income poverty and the severe hardship they face. It has worked because of continued increases in employment and because of increases in the tax credit entitlement of families with children. The strategy so far has produced demonstrably positive results, but to make further progress more policy effort is needed.

## Measuring progress beyond 2004/05

The 2004 Spending Review will be complete in July 2004. The priorities coming out of the review will determine the direction of policy over the next three to four years, a long way – chronologically at least – towards the second milestone of halving child poverty by 2010. We have thus far assumed a continuation of the current way in which child poverty is officially measured. The conclusions of a Department for Work and Pensions review of these, published a couple of days before Christmas, suggest this will not be the case.[10]

The change proposed will take effect after the first PSA[11] target year (2004/05). The next PSA will apparently rely on three new measures:

1. **Absolute low income:** measured by the number of children living in households with a before housing cost equivalised income of less than 60 per cent of the 1998/99 median income, uprated for inflation.
2. **Relative low income:** measured as poor if they live in a household with a before housing cost equivalised income of less than 60 per cent of the contemporary median.
3. **Material deprivation and low income combined:** measured as poor if they live in a household with a before housing costs equivalised income of less than 70 per cent of the contemporary median and if they lack material necessities and cannot afford them.

It is, as yet, unclear how these three measures will interact (ie, how you know when child poverty has been halved), only that child poverty has to be falling on each of the measures, so we do not know if there is some order of importance among them. The change has a substantial effect both on the overall number of children defined as poor and, therefore, on the level of policy effort required to halve child poverty.

The new measures mean a shift away from using both before and after housing costs income poverty figures to relying solely on before housing costs income figures. Housing is a large and fixed element of family spending and so failing to account for it gives a poorer understanding of the disposable income actually available to the household. Further, there is also the perverse effect that, under this regime, housing benefit payments will be included as income. Someone with high rent and housing benefit payments to cover some, or all, of it would therefore show up as having potentially quite a high income, even though they may experience quite a low one. Since more children are defined as poor after accounting for housing costs than before these are accounted for, the switch reduces the number of children defined as poor.

On the first – absolute low income – measure it is very likely that child poverty will show a sustained fall, since over time incomes and living standards typically improve in real terms. However, this unhelpfully moves us away from an understanding of poverty which relates incomes to current social norms (relative income poverty). Any conceptualisation of poverty needs to relate experience to that of mainstream society.

The second measure – the relative income measure – is the closest to the current PSA regime. Because of this, and because this is the measure used most often by research and for the purpose of international comparison, it is likely to remain the headline quoted figure. The changes made to this measure, compared with the pre-existing PSA measure, are quantifiable on the basis of the existing *Households Below Average Income* figures for 2001/02. The after housing costs income poverty figure (see Table 7.1) has been the one often quoted, though both the after and before housing costs are covered under the current PSA. The result from the old regime to that implied in the second measure is to reduce the headline child income poverty figure from 3.8 million to 2.9 million.[12]

The third measure combines a measure of relative income – again before housing costs – with one of the ability to own and afford necessities. This measure will require a composite to be constructed of various questions about access to, and ability to afford, various necessities. Although a list of questions to be included in the Family Resources Survey (the Department for Work and Pensions survey used to measure poverty) was provided with the conclusions to the review of measures, it was not made clear which would be included in the eventual measure. Neither will we have estimates on the numbers of children facing various forms of material deprivation (from the Family Resources Survey) until 2006, when the first results will be published. The list of necessities which may be included in this measure include various items related to housing quality, and this has been used in partial justification of dropping the after housing costs measures.[13] Given that the effect of the first two measures is to define fewer children as poor (and so make it easier to reach the halving target), it will be important that the precise construction of this third measure is sufficiently exacting to set a tough test for the Government.[14] The challenge is to reduce child poverty by ensuring substantial, sustained improvements in the lives of poorer children, not by a methodological sleight of hand.

## Winning the argument

Progress has been made and in general the Government should be loudly and openly proud of this success. Yet we have had strikingly little debate on the subject. Certainly we have a PSA target – the first on the list – but at the 2001 general election the Labour Party hardly pushed the child poverty debate. It appeared on page 27 of the *Manifesto* and neither did it make the *Goals for 2010* (despite the existence of a promise to halve child poverty by precisely this date) or the *25 Steps to a Better Britain*.[15] The Government has been good at engaging with interested parties in the poverty lobby, with academics and, to a degree, with those actually experiencing the detrimental effects of poverty and social exclusion. What it has not done is sold its argument to end child poverty in a wider, more public, debate. The importance of the task and the scale of the challenge require a more open dialogue from the government and for it to sell the importance of what it is doing. To do so would be in its own interests, for without it the Government is hardly likely to reap the rewards of the progress. As Ruth Lister has noted elsewhere 'doing good by stealth has the disadvantage of not being seen to be doing good.'[16]

There are problems which need to be addressed within the current approach – highlighted throughout this book – areas in which more work is needed if child poverty is to be halved and eventually ended. Extra spending is required, but that already committed has yielded positive results. The concern that open commitment to redistributive policy would be an electoral liability may be more grounded in political perception than it is in reality. Certainly, the interpretation is not born out by attitudinal data. Analysis of the latest British Social Attitudes Survey sheds some light on this. Bromley examines the results of a series of questions related to redistribution and to inequality.[17] She uses data collected in 2002 and notes strong support for the statement 'the gap between high and low incomes is too large'. Eighty-two per cent supported the statement overall, varying by political allegiance between 71 per cent (Conservatives) to 84 per cent (Labour). There was no apparent contentment that the existing distribution is acceptable, irrespective of political support. The debate here, however, is rather abstract and no indication is given of what might be done about this apparent injustice. In taking the analysis away from this abstraction (and using data from 2000) Bromley notes the following contradiction in the data:

- 58 per cent agree that the 'Government is responsible for reducing income inequality';
- 39 per cent believe that the 'Government should redistribute from rich to poor'.

These two statements are closely related: the principal way the Government might achieve the former is through the latter. The explanation given for the discordance is that perhaps people believe that there are non-redistributive ways of reducing income inequality (such as the minimum wage) or that it is the word 'redistribution' and not the concept of resource transfer that is unpopular. Both are probably true, but the critical point is that there is demonstrably high support for a progressive tax system. Using 1999 data, Bromley shows that three-quarters (76 per cent) of those questioned thought that those on high incomes should pay a larger share of their income in taxes compared with those on lower incomes. Only 20 per cent believed the share should be the same, leaving next to no people believing that the tax system should be regressive. The regressive action of taxes, such as VAT or council tax, does not square with this public view of a good society.

There is an important argument to be made and it needs to be made boldly. It cannot be taken for granted that this is a policy area too dangerous for politicians to talk about. The argument is timely, not simply for the Left but also for the Centre Right, which is showing more interest in issues of poverty and social exclusion.[18] It is almost taken for granted that more spending on health and education is necessary and justifiable – a direct result of the case for investment being made and made loudly. The same is needed for reductions in child poverty.

## Making further progress

This book ought to give not only an indication of progress but also some of the areas in which the function of policy is inadequate, those wanting improvement. This final section reflects on these in the context of the need to make substantial further reductions in child poverty. The analysis of the Department for Work and Pensions family and children's dataset by Alan Marsh and Sandra Vegeris (Chapter Five) gives us a clear message: redistribution works. Spending on tax credits and increases in employment have brought with them demonstrable improvements in the lives of the poorest children. The proportions facing income poverty and in situations of severe hardship have fallen.

The current 'work as the best form of welfare' strategy is premised on ever-increasing employment, underpinned by tax credit redistribution. The strategy has brought about demonstrable reductions in income poverty and material hardship but it is possible that the easiest wins have already been had. If the employment rate is to be pushed further then it will get progressively harder to achieve. This is not necessarily an argument that dissuades action in this direction, but rather one that cautions practical difficulty and one which suggests there may be natural limits to the current strategy. If it is not possible to generate further increases in the employment rate, or if we encounter recession, then further strain is placed on tax credits to deliver improvements in family income. This itself suggests a need for further substantial tax credit investment and raises the question as to whether this is compatible with other policy objectives (such as maintaining the incentives for those in employment to increase their hours of work).

Tax credits are themselves a substantial and complicated mechanism: progressive and means tested. As with other means-tested benefits there have come many difficulties, the quality of the administration being the first and most high profile. Certainly, this was not helped by the speedy implementation of the scheme by the Inland Revenue, an organisation which had little experience of handling benefit payments or dealing with lower-income families who could be made destitute by slow or inaccurate decision making. At time of writing, in March 2004, significant problems have come to CPAG's attention where tax credit overpayments[19] are being clawed back by the Inland Revenue out of an existing award, leaving lower-income families in serious financial difficulties. These problems would certainly have been exacerbated by implementation problems, but they are also a long-term feature of the tax credits' annual assessment period. The Inland Revenue needs to find a better way of dealing with its clients in the future – preventing serious overpayments building up and making the process of recouping any overpayments more sensitive to the needs and circumstance of tax credit recipients.

It is vital to ensure that all policy is pulling in the same direction to maximise the impact on reducing child poverty. Part of the underlying need is to ensure that all areas of government (national and devolved) have reducing child poverty as a priority ('mainstreaming the issue') and part of it is to ensure that other priorities do not conflict with this central importance. Neera Sharma brings out some of this conflict in her discussion of the social care agenda, which, at present, is not sufficiently poverty-focused. The title of a recent Green Paper, *Every Child Matters*,[20] highlights a particularly sharp contradiction: this is simply not the way in which all children are treated, either under the current system or under the system the Green Paper proposes. Sharma discusses the particular experiences of children of families seeking asylum, of disabled children, of children in temporary accommodation and of Black and ethnic minority children. In each case, she details the way in which children experience circumstances which are less favourable than the typical experience.

Underlying the 'work as the best form of welfare' policy emphasis is the development of childcare. In Chapter Four Lisa Harker demonstrates, however, that there are more reasons for having good-quality childcare than simply increasing labour supply – there are developmental gains for children also. Harker demonstrates the difficulties surrounding the childcare debate: both supply and demand. The childcare workforce is too small in this field and, understandably enough, is concentrated in the areas where the highest returns are to be made. This means that not only is there insufficient childcare overall, but that the limitation of supply is especially acute in more disadvantaged areas. There is, therefore, a case for saying that if we are to enjoy good-quality childcare of sufficient quantity, then costs must rise. Yet the cost to parents is already highlighted as prohibitive and a barrier to work in certain areas – leading to pressures for the 70 per cent cap on the costs of childcare in the childcare element of working tax credit to be increased. Rising costs of childcare need to be more than matched by government funding if this is to yield the advantages both in supply increases and in the ability of parents from lower income families to access it. Any such increase in funding would need to occur in such a way that it paid off in more affordable childcare, and not only in increased childcare costs.

Within recent policy debates and official pronouncements the phrase 'progressive universalism' has reverberated frequently. The phrase has been used to capture much of the essence of policy thrust – focused on those on lower incomes, but doing so in a way which captures a large proportion of the population. To the purist there is an inherent flaw in the concept – universal benefits, such as child benefit, deliver resources to all, not only those on lower incomes (although in a proportional sense they do target poorer people, as a fixed amount is worth most to those on the lowest income). Nevertheless this is a useful notion – benefits and services usually work best when they go to all, since the whole community has an interest in ensuring good quality. Such services are expensive, so there is clearly a balance to be struck. This concept may be seen to lie behind much policy, a good example being the way in which the tax credits go far up the income scale, but deliver most to those on the lowest incomes. However, although the majority of families may be entitled, the need for an assessment of income (exacerbated by scheme structure) has led to the administrative problems discussed above. The use of area-based approaches outlined by Pete Alcock also illustrates this tension. Focus policy on an area because of its deprivation and, although you may affect many of those who experience deprivation, you will not improve the lives of all in this situation: because not all demonstrably poor people live in demonstrably poor areas. Whatever the resource and political pros and cons, a more comprehensive approach to this is the universal model – income and services to all – which would avoid administrative problems of applying the means test to tax credits and of focusing on certain areas at the exclusion of others. Universalism needs to remain a substantial part of the approach for combating poverty.

In general, progress to date has been encouraging but there is a long way to go yet. To stay on track we will need much more redistribution towards poorer families with children. The UK (the fourth largest economy in the world) certainly has the resources for this, but the Government needs to demonstrate that it has the political will. We need much greater public awareness and public debate to support the necessary policies, driven by the Government and by interested parties like CPAG. Ending child poverty is morally right and technically feasible; it can be done and it should be done.

## Notes

1   Department for Work and Pensions, *Public Service Agreement (PSA) Technical Note for the Department for Work and Pensions*, Department for Work and Pensions and HM Treasury, 2002

2   The arithmetic process by which the different incomes are adjusted to account for different expenditure needs (the determining factors are the size of household and ages of children).

3   Data has been published as the Households Below Average Income series, but is generated from a national survey, the *Family Resources Survey*, which covers private households in the United Kingdom (although until 2001/02 this only covered Great Britain)

4   H Sutherland, T Sefton and D Piachaud, *Poverty in Britain: the impact of government policy since 1997*, Joseph Rowntree Foundation, 2003

5   M Brewer and G Kaplan, 'What do the Child Poverty Targets Mean for the Child Tax Credit?', in R Chote, C Emmerson and H Simpson (eds), *The IFS Green Budget*, Institute for Fiscal Studies, 2003; M Brewer, A Goodman and A Shephard, *How has Child Poverty Changed Under the Labour Government? An update*, Institute for Fiscal Studies, 2003; M Brewer, *What do the Child Poverty Targets Mean for the Child Tax Credit? An update*, Briefing Note 41, Institute for Fiscal Studies, 2003

6   Institute for Fiscal Studies, 'IFS Analysis: Pre-Budget Report Analysis', Press Release, December 2003

7   Institute for Fiscal Studies, IFS Pre-Budget Report presentation, see www.ifs.org.uk/budgetindex.shtml, 11 December 2003

8   See note 2, p63

9   HM Treasury, *Budget 2003*, HC 500, p105, para.5.10, April 2003

10  See Department for Work and Pensions, *Measuring Child Poverty DWP*, December 2003

11  See note 1

12  The difference is between the higher of the old relative income measures, 60 per cent of after housing costs equivalised household income (3.8 million children are measured as poor) and the new measure, 60 per cent of before housing costs equivalised household income, together with a change in the equivalisation formula (2.9 million children are measured as poor). See Office for National Statistics, *Households Below Average Income 1994/95–2001/02*, Department for Work and Pensions, 2003, pp65 and 258

13  See note 8, para 25

14  Jonathan Bradshaw has, for example, suggested fixing the baseline to measure the same number of children as poor under the new material deprivation measure as were categorised as poor under the old after housing costs PSA target. See http://www.psi.org.uk/docs/2004/JonathanBradshawSeminar.pdf

15  See Labour Party, *Ambitions for Britain: Labour's manifesto 2001*, 2001

16  Quoted by S Regan and P Robinson, 'Loud and Clear: an open and persistent poverty strategy', in Joseph Rowntree Foundation, *Overcoming Disadvantage*, Joseph Rowntree Foundation, 2004

17  See C Bromley, 'Has Britain Become Immune to Inequality?', in A Park, J Curtice, K Thomson, L Jarvice and C Bromley, *British Social Attitudes*, 20th report NatCen, 2003, pp71-92

18 See, for instance, a recent contribution to the Joesph Rowntree Foundation's report, from the right-of-centre think tank, Policy Exchange. See N Hillman, 'Condemning a Little Less and Understanding a Little More', in *Overcoming Disadvantage*, Joseph Rowntree Foundation, 2004

19 These occur because for all or part of the year entitlement information held by the Inland Revenue is inaccurate. This is exacerbated by the annual assessment period which allows overpayments to build up before being discovered, either by the Inland Revenue or by the claimant.

20 Department for Education and Skills, *Every Child Matters*, Department for Education and Skills, 2003